Twice She Struck

Twice She Struck

The Story of RMS *Rhone*

Michael D. Kent

Copyright © 2017 Michael D. Kent

All rights reserved

Twice She Struck- The Story of RMS *Rhone*

First Edition

Author: Michael D. Kent

ISBN-13: 9780995758407
ISBN-10: 0995758409
Library of Congress Control Number: 2017903966
Michael D. Kent, Miami, FL

No part of this book may be reproduced or transmitted in any form or by any means, either electronic or mechanical, without direct written permission from the author.

twiceshestruck@gmail.com

Cover photograph – Jonathan Bailey with the life ring that saved him (The Royal Society).

This book is dedicated to the memory of those people who lost their lives aboard RMS *Rhone* on October 29, 1867.

Table of Contents

Acknowledgments ix
List of Plates xi
Preface xv

Chapter 1 Colonisation and Communication 1
Chapter 2 The Royal Mail Steam Packet Company 8
Chapter 3 The Birth of *Rhone* 21
Chapter 4 "This Fairy Group of Islands" 31
Chapter 5 The Sinking of RMS *Rhone* 44
Chapter 6 Aftermath 56
Chapter 7 Earthquake and Tsunami 70
Chapter 8 Salvage and Rediscovery 82
Chapter 9 The Wreck Site Today 94

Sources 105

Acknowledgments

THE AUTHOR WOULD like to thank Dr. Charles Wheatley, OBE; Mr. Clive Petrovic; Mrs. Jennie Wheatley, MBE; Mr. George Wilkinson; Miss. Traci O'Dea; Mr. Joseph Smith-Abbott; Mrs. Nancy Woodfield-Pascoe; Alan and Eva Baskin; Mr. Armando Jenik; Katherine Marshall at the Royal Society; the staff of Hampshire Archives; and the staff at the National Maritime Museum.

List of Plates

1. The arrival of Columbus in the Americas in 1492 (Alamy). 3
2. Captain William Rogers capturing the *Jeune Richard*,
   October 1, 1807 (Alamy). 7
3. A Grenada plantation (Alamy). 9
4. RMS *Amazon* (Alamy). 13
5. RMS *Atrato* with the abandoned *Rover's Pride* in 1857 (Alamy). . . . 14
6. RMS *Parramatta* on the reef at Anegada (Alamy). 16
7. HMS *Rattler* towing the *Alecto* in 1845 (Alamy). 18
8. HMS *Warrior*, built in 1860 (Alamy). 19
9. The *Great Eastern* under construction at the J. Scott Russell
   and Company yard circa 1857 (Alamy). 23
10. One of the original 1864 Millwall Iron Works Ship
    Building & Graving Docks Company Ltd. share
    certificates (Author's collection). 24
11. The Millwall Iron Works Ship Building & Graving
    Docks Company Ltd. in 1864 (Alamy). 25
12. The men who built *Rhone* in 1864 (Alamy). 26
13. The loss of the steamship *London* in 1866 (Alamy). 28
14. The only known photograph of RMS *Rhone* afloat,
    circa 1866 (Hampshire Records Office). 29
15. The harbour of St. Thomas circa 1860s (Alamy). 34
16. Fireman stoking a ship's boiler (Alamy). 36
17. The *Rhone* and *Conway* rafted alongside each
    other prior to the storm (George Wilkinson). 37

18. The *Rhone* and *Conway* separate at the beginning of the storm (George Wilkinson). 39
19. Chief Officer Dalby Topper killed by a falling spar (George Wilkinson). 40
20. The *Rhone* steaming for open water (George Wilkinson). 41
21. The *Rhone* approaching Black Rock Point, Salt Island (George Wilkinson). 42
22. The *Rhone* strikes Black Rock Point at approximately 2:00 p.m. (George Wilkinson). 44
23. The *Rhone* breaks up (George Wilkinson). 47
24. Crew members cling to the fore top yard (George Wilkinson). 49
25. Damaged ships in St. Thomas Harbour, October 30, 1867 (Alamy). 57
26. The *Rhone*'s forward mast the following morning (George Wilkinson). 62
27. Jonathan Bailey with fellow surviving cabin boy John Minns (the Royal Society). 67
28. The *Rhone* and *Wye* monument in the Old Cemetery, Southampton (Alamy). 69
29. *La Plata* riding the tsunami bore (Alamy). 76
30. After the tsunami in St. Thomas harbour (Alamy). 81
31. The *Rhone* cemetery on Salt Island (Junior Daniel). 87
32. Bert Kilbride with some of the artefacts he salvaged from *Rhone* (Eva Baskin). 90
33. Jacqueline Bisset, Nick Nolte, and Robert Shaw filming the 1977 movie *The Deep* (Alamy). 91
34. Black Rock Point today (Junior Daniel). 92
35. The bow section of the *Rhone* resting on the starboard side (Armando Jenik). 94
36. The *Rhone*'s cannon pointing out through the wreckage (Armando Jenik). 98

37. Squirrel fish gathering around the condenser (Armando Jenik). 98
38. A Nurse shark drifting through the wreckage (Armando Jenik). 99
39. The *Rhone*'s propeller (Armando Jenik). 101
40. A diver exploring the wreck of the *Rhone* (Alamy). 104

Preface

THE PUBLIC FASCINATION for shipwrecks is seemingly inexhaustible. Even the most practical person, when confronted with the subject, drifts into a surreal fantasy world, dreaming of doubloons and pear-size rubies locked within a wooden chest, encased amongst the ruined timbers of a Spanish galleon lying upright on the Caribbean seabed.

A variety of books and websites tout the top ten shipwrecks in the world, mentioning such legends as the SS *Thistlegorn* in Egypt, the *Rainbow Warrior* in New Zealand, the USS *Saratoga* in the Marshall Islands, and the *Zenobia* in Cyprus. Most are similar in their choices, and all of them contain one shipwreck that still captures the imagination of thousands of divers annually. The RMS *Rhone* sank in 1867 during appalling weather conditions with a heavy loss of life. She was a very early example of a single-screw iron-hull passenger vessel and was considered one of the most advanced ships afloat when launched two years earlier. A variety of conditions make her a premium dive site, including the intact state of the hull, her mid-nineteenth-century design, the tragic story surrounding her loss, her accessibility to divers and snorkelers, the beautiful Caribbean waters that encompass her, and the exotic marine life that now inhabits her.

My personal interest in the *Rhone* began in 1994 when, as a young diving instructor, I arrived in the British Virgin Islands (BVI) and began visiting the wreck site daily. As a child, I had always been fascinated by shipwrecks and can remember a picture I painted at boarding school in Worcestershire illustrating two divers descending to the seabed, where an abandoned ship sat beside a large treasure chest. I must have been no older than ten at the time. Many years later, I became immersed in the story surrounding *Rhone* and her demise, which I would recount to visiting divers during surface intervals before guiding them around the stern portion of the wreck.

As much as I appreciated the mystery and allure of *Rhone*, everything changed for me in September 1995. Two destructive hurricanes swept through the Virgin Islands, and the second of the two, Hurricane Marilyn, caused particularly bad damage to the BVI and, curiously, swept the seabed surrounding the wreck of the *Rhone*, revealing previously buried structural features. Likewise, a variety of artefacts began to appear, lying in full view, some of which were removed illegally and then extracted from the territory by visiting divers.

My frustration at seeing the loss of these items (which belonged in a BVI museum) led me to commit the biggest mistake of my life. I personally began collecting artefacts whenever I observed them and took them ashore to conduct what little amateur conservation work I could. I made no secret of what I was doing and showed the items I had collected to whoever was interested. Eventually, word reached the relevant authorities, and I was arrested on the dock and then taken to my apartment where I voluntarily handed over the collection. After being escorted to the police station, I was formally charged with removing artefacts from a national park and remanded in custody. I spent the night in a rancid, old cell, the perfect setting for a very uncomfortable and sobering experience. My then partner, Kelsey Dawn Fischer, brought me a book called *Maritime Archaeology* by Keith Mukelroy that had been lent to me by a friend. With nothing better to do, I sat in my cell and read the book from cover to cover. Twice. I then discovered that there was a legitimate professional method to achieve what I had attempted, and my future course was set.

I pled guilty to all the charges, paid the five-hundred-dollar fine, and was released. I had resigned from my dive instructor job in the BVI, so I returned to England and enrolled in a master's degree course at the University of Bristol, studying maritime archaeology. I returned to the BVI again in 1997 to conduct the fieldwork necessary to complete my degree under the watchful eye of the then president of H. Lavity Stoutt Community College (HLSCC) on Tortola, Dr. Charles Wheatley, and the head of marine sciences, Mr. Clive Petrovic. In 1998, I returned permanently to the BVI to work at HLSCC, where I joined the newly evolving Virgin Islands Studies Institute. My presence in the territory is a testament to the empathetic and compassionate nature of the BVI population, to whom I humbly and unreservedly apologise. I broke one of your laws, which was wrong, and I appreciate you giving me a second chance.

I have subsequently spent the last twenty years discovering, recording, documenting, and disseminating the historical sites remaining in the BVI both above and below water. A mistake I made as a young man stimulated me to study an enormously rich and diverse culture with a heroic history that is inspirational. In turning this page, I hope the reader is encouraged to do the same.

CHAPTER 1

Colonisation and Communication

THE ARRIVAL OF Christopher Columbus in the Bahamian archipelago on October 12, 1492, triggered a series of events that would dramatically change the course of European history permanently. It has been conjectured that the pre-Columbian Amerindian population of the Americas in 1492 may well have exceeded fifty million people, so to declare that Columbus discovered the continent is counterfactual. Likewise, excavations and dating at L'Anse-aux-Meadows in Newfoundland, Canada, categorically prove that a Scandinavian Norse settlement existed there around circa 950–1050, some five hundred years before Columbus, confirming a much earlier European occupation in the Americas. What Columbus did achieve was a permanent presence in the Western Hemisphere on behalf of his sponsors, King Ferdinand and Queen Isabella of Spain, which consolidated the freshly evolving concept of empirical expansion and colonisation.

Osterhammel, in his tome entitled *Colonialism*, states, "Colonisation designates a process of territorial acquisition, 'colony' a particular type of socio-political organisation, and 'colonialism' a system of domination. The basis of all three concepts is the notion of expansion of a society beyond its original habitat. These processes of expansion are a fundamental phenomenon of world history." By the end of the fifteenth century, the boundaries of the various European monarchies had been tentatively established, promoting a shift from the traditional medieval practice of wealth accumulation through conquest and plunder to the more subtle and contemporary pursuit of international trade.

Easily one of the most lucrative trade routes at this time was the Spice Trade, which had existed since 3000 BCE and later involved the transportation of rare agricultural commodities from Asia and North Africa to Europe. This commercial artery was highly competitive and contributed substantially towards the construction of Venice, whose merchants essentially controlled the European entrepôt for the various tropical goods. The Portuguese, in an effort to circumvent the Venetian domination, began to explore the African coastline with the aim of finding a maritime route to the source of the Spice Trade. In doing so, they created the first post-medieval European colonies when they landed in Madeira in 1419, which they settled a year later, and then subsequently the Azores in 1427.

Circumstances changed dramatically in 1453 when Mehmed II captured Constantinople, transforming the Ottoman state into a powerful empire, which effectively cut off Venetian access to the Spice Trade, making it essential to find another route to the source. This catalyst encouraged contemporary enlightened scholars to seriously begin suggesting the possibility of crossing the Great Ocean to reach Asia, a concept first proposed by Paolo dal Pozzo Toscanelli in 1474. Columbus, by this time, had sailed extensively along the traditional European trade routes and had dedicated himself to independent rather than formal education, allowing him freedom from the traditional confines of intellectual thought that dictated a southeast maritime route to Asia. By the early 1480s, he had adopted Toscanelli's proposal and began promoting his radical trans-Atlantic theory to the various European courts in an effort to gain financial support. He approached the Portuguese court and was refused twice in 1485 and 1488. Likewise, the English, Genoese, and Venetians all denied him patronage. When Ferdinand and Isabella finally agreed to provide him with an allowance in 1489, it was not because they believed he was necessarily correct, but more to make sure that other European polities were denied his ideas. Three years later, their intuition proved correct.

The arrival of Columbus in the Americas in 1492 (Alamy).

The initial Spanish colonisation of the Caribbean islands was a haphazard affair negatively influenced by individual greed, internal political jealousies, and traditional class struggles. The ratification of Spanish rights to the region granted by Pope Alexander VI in 1494 did, however, grant a trading monopoly beyond a specific line of demarcation to both Spain and Portugal at the exclusion of all other nations, creating an economic imbalance within Europe. The vast wealth in gold and silver that began to pour into the Spanish treasury during the opening of the sixteenth century encouraged French Corsairs to attack Havana successfully in 1538, prompting the demand for a regular protected supply convoy to leave from Spain twice a year for the Americas known as the Flota de Indias. Operating between 1566 and 1790, these fleets of cargo ships shadowed by their military counterparts left from Seville in Spain, providing a vital commercial artery and communications network between the mother country and her colonies. The returning fleet left from

Veracruz, Portobelo, or Cartagena, carrying precious metals, gems, pearls, tobacco, and sugar back to the Casa de Contratación in Seville, shifting the European pendulum of power in favour of the Spanish. In order to counteract this imbalance, Spain's traditional enemies began to challenge Iberian superiority in the Americas by sending predatory expeditions to the area designed to challenge the trading monopoly granted by the Borgia pope. Two of the most successful antagonists towards Spanish domination were the English mariners Francis Drake and John Hawkins.

Initial English involvement in the Caribbean region had revolved around harrying Spanish trade as much as possible, and, if possible, capturing some of the vast hordes of precious metals before they could be disgorged into the vaults of Seville. Drake and Hawkins had achieved both, much to the chagrin of the Spanish crown, which in the case of El Draque had offered a massive reward for his capture. As Spanish domination began to decline in Europe, especially after the defeat of the Armada sent to invade England in 1588, it occurred to the rookery of politicians in London who created foreign policy that it would be an opportune time to not only challenge trade in the Caribbean region, but also consider occupying some of the islands outright. With this in mind, Sir Thomas Warner was dispatched to the island of St. Christopher (St. Kitts) where, in 1623, he settled the first colony of what would exponentially grow into the British West Indies. Barbados was settled in 1627, and a year later, when Warner felt comfortable enough to spare some of his own colonists, he allowed Thomas Hilton to occupy neighbouring Nevis. Antigua and Montserrat were subsequently annexed in 1632, creating a permanent and profitable presence in the Eastern Caribbean. These new Caribbean settlements required a regular correspondence between the metropolitan capital, London, and the newly occupied frontier societies in order to maintain trade and sovereignty in colonies that were highly contested by other European courts.

Embryonic English settlements had been organised by private patent holders with the expectation that they would converse with and supply their own individual dominions. The home government hesitated to commit public resources towards a reliable communications network due to the lack of any official colonial policy and the indifferent political status of the quasi-developed plantation islands. Further conflict at the beginning of the eighteenth century compounded this situation when private vessels consistently fell prey to enemy warships and privateers, considerably disrupting an already unreliable mail service between Britain and the West Indies.

Whilst not prepared to operate a regular packet service itself, the British government was not adverse to others attempting to try, so it supported an idea proposed by Edmund Dummer in 1702. His proposal would provide "terms for settling a monthly intelligence between England and the island plantations in the West Indies." Lord Nottingham approved the plan in August of that year, and in November, the treasury issued a warrant to the postmaster general authorising payment of £2,000 to Dummer for "four fit sloops or vessels to go out monthly from Falmouth to the West India Islands, according to your contract with him for a constant correspondence between England and the said islands for the encouragement and benefit of trade."

Though essentially sound, Dummer's idea involved too much capital risk for one person to absorb. During his nine years of operation, he lost ten ships to enemy action whilst two just disappeared at sea. Consequently, by the end of 1711, the service had ceased, and Dummer was bankrupt.

The introduction of sugarcane agriculture dramatically accelerated expansion of the British West Indian colonies during the early 1700s. The 4 percent duty demanded by the crown from each of the colonies as a remittance for the privilege of legislative government encouraged the planters to petition the Lords of Trade and Plantations for a regular packet service to be reintroduced. Continuous pressure from the powerful West India merchants and a period of peace between 1748 and 1756 allowed the government time for reflection on the matter. In response, the postmaster general signed a contract in November 1755 for "carrying on a correspondence by four Packet Boats to and from the West Indies," beginning a utility that lasted until 1841.

Speed, reliability and strength characterised the packet service, which operated for eighty-six years. The ships, based at Falmouth in Cornwell, were required to be over 150 tons each and manned by sixteen officers and men. Due to the importance of their cargo, each was obliged to be armed with "eight carriage and six swivel guns, with proper ammunition." Initially, the ships operated two routes, and, apart from accommodating more stops, they remained virtually the same throughout the service. The American route stopped first at New York and then proceeded to New England, Virginia, Maryland, and all other colonies on the continent of North America whilst the West Indian route stopped first at Barbados and from there proceeded to Antigua, Montserrat, Nevis, St. Christopher, and Jamaica.

This route later included Tortola, where the military strength of a packet ship was illustrated in February 1794. Having received intelligence that a force of three French privateers intended an attack on Tortola, the president of the council, George Leonard, detained Captain Curzon of the packet *Queen Charlotte* at Road Harbour in order to supplement the town's defences with the ship's battery of guns. Leonard defended his decision by stating that he was "well aware of the particular delicacy with which the discretionary power of a Civil Commander to detain a packet ought to be exercised, and nothing but the extreme urgency of the case could, or would have induced me to use it upon this occasion as I was actuated by the best motives."

Enemy privateers infested the Northern Leeward Islands during this time, and on another occasion in 1807, after the heavily outgunned packet *Windsor Castle* engaged and defeated the French privateer *Jeune Richard*, the residents of Tortola presented the captain, William Rogers, with a sword of honour in gratitude.

By the early nineteenth century, the plantations of the British West Indian Islands experienced an irreversible economic decline making regular communications less necessary. In 1834, Britain abolished slavery and introduced a system of apprenticeship for freed slaves until 1838. Shortly thereafter, plantations could no longer function without the free labour upon which they had relied in the past.

The introduction of steamships heralded the end of the sailing packets, and in 1840, the government signed a contract with a fledgling private enterprise that proposed to take over the West Indies postal contract. The company was the brainchild of Scottish entrepreneur James MacQueen and christened the Royal Mail Steam Packet Company (RMSPC).

Captain William Rogers capturing the *Jeune Richard*, October 1, 1807 (Alamy).

CHAPTER 2

The Royal Mail Steam Packet Company

THE FOUNDER OF the Royal Mail Steam Packet Company, James MacQueen, was born in 1779 near the small village of Crawford in Lanarkshire, Scotland, close to the source of the River Clyde. He grew up in a Scotland, which for over half a century had been gradually dominated by the British King-in-Parliament, a process that had begun with the death of the last Tudor, Elizabeth I (1533–1603), who had passed without issue. Due to the lack of any heir to succeed the Virgin Queen, the English crown automatically reverted to James VI of Scotland (1566–1625) on the basis that his great-grandmother was the eldest sister of Henry VIII (1491–1547). Consequently, the two kingdoms, whilst still retaining separate parliaments, were ruled by the same monarch, a man whose primary ambition was to amalgamate both together under one banner. This failed to take place during his reign, but eventually occurred in 1707 during the reign of Queen Anne (1665–1714) with the Act of Union that united both kingdoms into Great Britain.

Many Scottish clansmen despised losing their autonomy and fuelled by a desire to replace the Hanoverian British King George II (1683–1760), rallied under the flag of Charles Edward Stewart, more affectionately known as Bonny Prince Charlie. The subsequent Jacobite Rebellion that ignited in 1745 was decisively crushed at the Battle of Culloden near Inverness on April 16, 1746, during which the Hanoverian forces commanded by the Duke of Cumberland routed an army consisting mostly of Highlanders from a variety of clans. In order to escape the subsequent repressive tyranny and encouraged by opportunities abroad in the Caribbean, some 17,000 Scots migrated to the region between 1750 and 1800, including James MacQueen, who arrived in Grenada during 1797.

A Grenada plantation (Alamy).

MacQueen landed on the island just one year after the suppression of a localised rebellion led by a man named Julien Fedon, a free mulatto of French extraction who owned a coffee and cocoa plantation called Belvedere Estate. Up until 1763, Grenada had been a French colony until it was begrudgingly ceded to the British during the Treaty of Paris at the end of the Seven Years War (1756–63). Emboldened by the celebrated French Revolutionary Victor Hugues, Fedon, on the premise of returning the island to Gallic rule, gathered together some one hundred free blacks and slaves and then fell upon the village of Grenville, slaughtering eleven of the fifteen white inhabitants. Having plundered all of the store houses, the rebels burnt the settlement to the ground and then marched to join other insurgents who had mustered to their cause. A protractedly vicious conflict followed, lasting for fifteen months and resulting in damage estimated at £2.5 million. The buildings and works on sixty-five estates were destroyed, the crops for 1794, 1795, and 1796 were lost, and seven thousand slaves were killed. It was amidst this chaos and confusion that MacQueen arrived on the devastated Westerhall Estate where he received a salary of £40 per annum to revive productivity.

The next thirteen years saw MacQueen assimilate into plantation life whilst travelling extensively throughout the Caribbean. Though he never visited Africa, he developed a profound fascination for the continent, which he discussed at great length with the Mandingo slaves under his charge. He likewise found inspiration from the books detailing the adventures of Scottish explorer Mungo Parke, who had discovered the source of the Niger in 1796. MacQueen projected fourteen years before it was proved by Landers that the Niger exited into the Atlantic somewhere in the vicinity of the Benin and Biafra bights, and it was probably for this reason he was elected a Fellow of the Royal Geographical Society.

In many ways an oxymoronic character, MacQueen was a fierce anti-abolitionist who also studied the practicality of organised trade as a means to eliminating African slavery. Like many other people familiar with the West Indian plantation system, he feared the consequences of abolition on the basis that an economic and social system that had remained intact for nearly two centuries would collapse, presenting unknown repercussions for Britain. Likewise, George Canning, who served briefly as the prime minister during the twilight years of British slavery, stated during his tenure as secretary of state in the mid-1820s:

> If I am asked whether I am for the permanent existence of slavery in our colonies, I say no. But if I am asked whether I am favourable to its immediate abolition, I say, no. And if I am asked which I would prefer, permanent slavery or abolition, I do not know whether under all the perplexing circumstances of the case, I must not say, I would prefer things remaining as they are. God knows! Not from any love of the existing state of things,

but on account of the tremendous responsibility of attempting to mend it.

This old argument had been used by Henry Dundas when, as home secretary in 1792, he counteracted William Wilberforce's Bill to Abolish the Slave Trade by suggesting a gradual abolition on the basis that any sudden dislocation of the system would prove disastrous for the colonial economies. These countermaneuvers manufactured by the powerful West India lobby were eventually quashed, but as far as MacQueen was concerned, addressed only one of the issues effecting perennial trade with the West Indies. Having accepted the inevitability of abolition, and on the basis that any commodity manufactured or grown in the region had to be transported to Europe, MacQueen began to focus his attention on the issue of reliable shipping and a regular commercial maritime communication service between Britain and the Caribbean islands. He embraced maritime steam technology as an alternative to what had towards its end become an undependable utility precariously operated by the home government.

By the early 1800s, steam-driven vessels had become more prolific and reliable, leading MacQueen to the conclusion that they could potentially be used to maintain a dependable source of transportation between Britain and her expanding empire. On his return to Glasgow in 1830, MacQueen became part owner of a newspaper but still gestated his dreams of creating a Royal Mail line of steamers. Seven years later, MacQueen publicly presented his ideas, which Parliament favourably received. During January 1838, he approached the Treasury with his proposal, which led to an agreement by the government-sponsored West India Committee to find the necessary financial backing. In July the following year, the directors of the RSMPC held their first meeting in the counting house of the merchant bankers Reid, Irving & Co. in Tokenhouse Yard, London. As a direct consequence of this meeting, MacQueen was appointed general superintendent of affairs with an authorised share capital of £1,500,000. Later in 1839, Queen Victoria granted a royal charter incorporating the company, and in March 1840, the Lords of the Admiralty signed a contract for the carriage of mail to the British Caribbean islands. Within a month, the company had commissioned a variety of shipyards to build fourteen steamers, and the fleet was born.

The schooners *Lee* and *Liffey* sailed first, taking up their local stations in the Caribbean. On January 3, 1842, the *Thames* and *Tay* sailed from Falmouth with the mail for the first time. *Thames* headed for Berbice, Havana, New York, and Halifax whilst the *Tay* set a course for Barbados. Built in different yards as a hedge against individual delay, the identical first fifteen ships were 275 feet long with a berth of 60 feet over the paddle boxes. Weighing 1,841 gross tons, they were powered by a simple side lever two-cylinder four hundred horsepower nominal engine, capable of driving the wooden hull at nine knots by eight-foot-long paddles fashioned from birch wood. Supporting the primitive engine, sails were rigged in the fashion of a three-masted barquentine with only the foremast square rigged. The ships had one hundred cabins and cost a total of £60,000 apiece.

Although the science of navigation had advanced dramatically with the introduction of the marine chronometer in the late eighteenth century and more accurate charts in the nineteenth century, the numerous reefs that litter the Gulf of Mexico and Caribbean basin began to take their toll early on the RMSPC. The organisation experienced its first loss in May 1842, after just five months of operating, when the *Medina* was wrecked at Turks Island. Captain Burnley managed to save all 64 passengers and 104 crew, but the ship was a complete loss. Five months later, having sustained damage at Puerto Rico, the *Isis* foundered near Bermuda, leaving the company in the precarious position of having no vessels to deliver the mail. In April the following year, the *Solway* fell victim to poor navigational aids at Corunna with the deaths of seventeen passengers and eighteen crew. Having been in business just one year, the RMSPC had lost ships valued at £53,668 and had a trading deficit of £70,790. On a positive note, the RMSPC switched its base of operations to

Southampton (far more convenient than Falmouth), where it remained for the duration of the company's existence.

Tragedy struck again on January 3, 1852, mere hours after the *Amazon*, the largest English-built paddle ship to date at her launch in June the previous year, set sail on her maiden voyage from Southampton. After rounding Portland Bill at approximately 9:00 p.m., crew members noticed that the paddles were overheating so doused them with water whilst greasing the bearings to decrease friction. Just after midnight, the second officer noticed flames coming from the forward hold but, beaten back by the heat, could not reach the ship's controls and stop the engines. Consequently, *Amazon*, ablaze, steamed on into the night at nine knots with 162 souls aboard. Although typically impossible for the crew to launch the lifeboats whilst underway, they dispatched three, with fifty-eight people aboard. Captain Symons managed to push the last boat away, even though his clothes were on fire. Then, with all of his officers, sixty-eight crew, and thirty-six passengers, he slipped beneath the frigid English Channel with his ship, leaving only an audible hiss as the red-hot funnel made contact with the ice-cold winter water.

RMS *Amazon* (Alamy).

Initially, when the mail contract had been signed by the Admiralty, it had required wooden ships, which their Lordships insisted upon. The *Amazon* incident, however, persuaded them to change their minds, and from that time, all new RMSPC vessels were made of iron.

A period of rapid expansion characterised the following few years for the RMSPC with a variety of vessels being commissioned, in particular the *Conway*, which was specifically designed for the West Indies route. Built by William Pitcher of Northfleet in Kent, she was 215 feet long and capable of reaching a speed of nine knots. In 1853, the *Conway* had a lucky escape after losing her rudder and consequently the ability to manoeuvre after she struck the rocks at Belltate Point on St. Kitts.

The fleet was supplemented by new technology in 1853 with the launches of the *Atrato* and *Wye*. The first purpose-built iron-hulled vessel for the RMSPC, the *Atrato* became the largest steamer in the world when finished. She was more famous, however, for an incident that occurred in 1857, when whilst at sea she spotted the vessel *Rover's Pride* in apparent distress. Upon approaching the fully rigged ship, the crew of *Atrato* noticed that *Rover's Pride* was unmanned, having been abandoned by her crew, and featured a homemade nest in the mizzen mast, which indicated that someone had survived and hidden there for a long period of time.

RMS *Atrato* with the abandoned *Rover's Pride* in 1857 (Alamy).

Paddle-wheel technology by the mid-nineteenth century had reached an apogee, and between 1858 and 1860, the RMSPC constructed three twin-side paddle iron-hulled leviathans named *Parramatta, Shannon,* and *Seine*. The first of these, *Parramatta,* constructed at the Thames Iron Works, stretched 330 feet long, weighed 2,166 tons, and had a crew of 120 serving the ship and her 160 passengers. At her launch on November 8, 1858, she rolled violently as she entered the water, almost capsizing. For the superstitious, this may have served as a portent for what followed on her maiden voyage.

Parramatta left Southampton for the first and last time on June 17, 1859, with a full complement of passengers and crew. Her Atlantic crossing passed relatively uneventfully apart from an incident on June 24, when her starboard paddle struck what was later established as flotsam, damaging one of the floats (paddles) and an iron stay connecting the ribs to the floats. This delayed the ship for six hours but did not otherwise interfere with the navigation of the vessel. As she approached the West Indies, sightings were taken to establish her position in order to steer her past Sombrero Island towards the safety of her destination, St. Thomas.

At 6:56 p.m. on June 30, *Parramatta*'s chief officer, Mr. Scrimger, on lookout, hailed from the masthead that Sombrero Island had been sighted on the southern bow, and the course was altered. A few minutes later, the chief officer confessed that what he had seen was in fact a vessel under sail rather than Sombrero; however, Captain Baynton, against strict company instructions, carried on steaming ahead at 12.5 knots rather than slowing down and establishing his position during daylight. At 7:25 p.m., both the captain and chief officer took another reading, but the horizon was now hazy and they both doubted the accuracy of their position. To compound the situation, Captain Baynton then ordered the third officer, Mr. Thissleton, to take a reading, but his did not agree with either of the previous two. At 9:27 p.m., Baynton, who was by this time completely confused as to exactly where his ship was located, went below to consult his charts. Before he reached the companion where his cabin was located, the ship struck the Horseshoe Reef at Anegada and held fast to a large tabletop coral head, rejecting any attempts to run her astern from the obstruction. Those aboard subsequently abandoned the ship.

RMS *Parramatta* on the reef at Anegada (Alamy).

Although extensive efforts were made to recover *Parramatta*, they were to no avail, and she was relinquished to the Horseshoe Reef. At the subsequent enquiry held at the Greenwich Police Court in London during December 1859, the court found Captain Baynton at fault for ignoring company instructions, and he was dismissed from the RMSPC. As further punishment, the court suspended his Masters Certificate of Competency for twelve months, denying him the ability to earn a living. In a letter to the Lords Privy Council for Trade written on New Year's Eve 1859, Baynton begged his superiors to allow him a certificate as chief mate in order to support his family during his period of suspension. In a heartfelt plea, he pointed out, "Whatever view your Lordships may take of the matter, I can assure you the loss of so fine a ship, combined with the necessity of commencing a new career after 16 years faithful service in the Royal Mail Company, is sufficient punishment to any man possessed of the smallest degree of feeling."

One week later, in early January 1860, Baynton received a letter from the Office of the Committee of Privy Council for Trade informing him that his request for a chief mate's ticket had been approved, allowing him to continue working as a professional mariner.

Although the *Parramatta* incident had profoundly embarrassed the board of directors at the RMSPC, it failed to dampen the company's enthusiasm for expansion, which it vigorously pursued throughout the following decade. In 1860, Charles Dickens completed his novel *Great Expectations*, the title of which aptly reflected the philosophy of the British people during this period of technical and scientific acceleration. Colonial expansion advanced rapidly, emphasising the necessity for more reliable means of communication both home and abroad. In 1863, the first underground railway was completed in London, stretching from Piccadilly to Farringdon Street, whilst in January the following year, Charing Cross station opened, facilitating easier access to the metropolis from some of the more remote agrarian shires and counties of the English countryside.

Across the Atlantic, the international rapture for modernisation was tainted by the perennial issue of slavery that still plagued American society, creating bitter divisions. Tensions combusted in December 1860 when South Carolina seceded from the Union rapidly followed within two months by Mississippi, Florida, Alabama, Georgia, Louisiana, and Texas. The following April, a force of Confederates, under General Pierre Beauregard, opened fire with fifty cannons on Fort Sumter at Charleston, South Carolina, heralding the outbreak of the American Civil War. Politicians in Westminster, recognising the negative diplomatic consequences of involvement, declared neutrality and pledged not to become embroiled on either side. This relief from conflict buoyed the British people's morale, which was dampened just months later by the death of Prince Albert, after which the nation was plunged into indefinite mourning by his widow Queen Victoria.

In order for the RMSPC not to default on the mail contract, the company completed another vessel to the same specifications of *Parramatta* as her replacement. In 1860, the RMSPC launched the *Seine*, and she immediately embarked on the Caribbean routes originally intended for her short-lived sister.

For the next four years, the company carefully monitored the evolution of marine steam propulsion as paddle wheels were slowly rendered obsolete being replaced by the propeller. The concept of screw propulsion had existed in a variety of forms since Archimedes (287–212 BC) but only really became practicable for ocean-going vessels in the mid-nineteenth century. The accolade of inventor is contentious, but is generally accredited to Francis Pettit Smith and John Ericsson, both of whom obtained a patent for a marine propeller in 1835. Subsequent development was rapid, resulting in 1840 with the application and approval of a patent for a conoidal propeller invented by George Rennie. Rennie recognised that by amalgamating the concepts of increased pitch, multiple threads, and minimum convolutions, a more efficient configuration was achievable, resulting in a design from which modern-day propellers trace their evolution.

In common with most vessel refinements, merchant fleets procrastinated change until the Royal Navy conducted trials and endorsed new ideas. Only then would they adopt these changes into their own commercial *modus operandi*. During a characteristically boisterous experiment in 1845, the Admiralty staged a tug-of-war competition between the *Rattler*, a propeller-driven ship, and the *Alecto*, a paddle steamer. Predictably, the former won, towing the latter astern at a consistent 2.5 knots.

HMS *Rattler* towing the *Alecto* in 1845 (Alamy).

During the following decade, the Royal Navy experimented further with the concept of screw propulsion, culminating in HMS *Warrior*. News had reached the Admiralty in 1858 that the French planned to construct an iron-clad warship named *Le Gloire*, which they subsequently completed in 1859. By response, the *Warrior* was commissioned, and when launched in 1860, rendered every other battleship in the world obsolete. A remaining testimony to her conceptual design records that during *Warrior*'s ten-year front-line service history, she was never attacked, primarily because of her superior strength and manoeuvrability. The single-expansion, propeller-driven engine that powered her proved far more practical than paddle wheels, owing to greater efficiency, a less complex power transmission system, and drastically reduced susceptibility to damage during a military engagement.

HMS *Warrior*, built in 1860 (Alamy).

Despite the apparent advantages of screw propulsion, a number of implementation problems lingered before the concept could be universally applied to merchant fleets. Amongst these included heavy vibration under steam (capable of shaking a wooden ship to pieces), making expensive iron vessels mandatory. This necessitated a comprehensive revaluation of hull design and composition and the addition of thrust bearings that conducted the force exerted by the propeller to the hull. Although submerged propellers had clear advantages over paddle wheels, they were only effective at high speeds, making the design of more powerful engines necessary, which fostered revolutionary techniques for casting and machining tougher compositions of metal. Once these hurdles had been overcome, the future of iron-hulled, propeller-driven vessels was assured, and subsequently, the timid shipping companies slowly adopted the new innovations.

CHAPTER 3

The Birth of *Rhone*

THE ROYAL MAIL Steam Packet Company had tampered with the inevitable changes steam engines presented by purchasing *Oneida*, a single-screw iron vessel, from the Canada Ocean Steam Ship Company in 1856. Ideas had been drifting around the company boardroom about how to reinspire public confidence after Captain Baynton's debacle at Anegada. One suggestion was the fleet's inclusion of two new ships capable of stunning potential passengers with their speed, luxury, and reliability. These new vessels would have to encompass the zenith of mid-nineteenth-century maritime technology, incorporating screw propulsion within a riveted iron hull. Concentrating primarily on first-class passengers, their interior accommodations would be designed to furnish patrons with a decadence rarely seen outside of an English stately home.

Once the decision had been taken and a vote cast, the team of chosen designers sought two capable shipyards to appoint with the construction of their dual dream. After considerable investigation, they identified two outfits, one in Scotland, the other in England. In common with all company vessels, the two new additions would be named after famous major rivers. The first, *Douro*, would be built by Caird and Company in Greenock, Scotland, and named after the iconic Portuguese river; the second, *Rhone*, would be built by the Millwall Iron Works in London and named after the famous French watercourse. In 1863, work started on the new steamers amidst great public anticipation.

British overseas expansion had demanded an expeditious increase in shipyards capable of producing reliable vessels, and the natural core for this industry was London, where direct access to the sea via the Thames was supplemented by a myriad of metropolitan contacts capable of purveying materials from around the globe. Within the capitol, one area stood alone, surrounded by water on three sides, almost forming an island, being semi-enclosed by the largest meander weaving through the ancient city. Because Edward III (1312–1377) had used this confined area to kennel his greyhounds, it became known as the Isle of Dogs, a name first recorded in 1520. The gusting winds that blasted through the Thames provided fuel for sail vessels and, during the medieval period, had also encouraged the construction of windmills along the river's edge. An embankment wall was built in order to support the heavy mill towers. In time, this stretch of the Thames became known as Millwall, and it was here in 1835 that the famous Scottish engineer, William Fairbairn, laid out an iron foundry on a three-acre site, giving birth to the Millwall Iron Works.

Fairbairn's primary concentration was the structural integrity of iron, and it was for this research and his contribution to engineering in general that he was eventually knighted in 1869. It was hull construction, however, which paid the bills, and more than one hundred ships, mostly under two thousand tons, were built by Fairbairn at Millwall, including vessels for the Admiralty, the merchant marine, the tsar of Russia, and the king of Denmark. The yard was concentrated around an impressive 150-foot-tall chimney, designed to extract smoke through underground ducts from furnaces throughout the premises.

By 1845, Fairbairn's dream proved financially unprofitable and required a capital injection by John Scott Russell who, as well as building ships there, also manufactured sugarcane crushing machinery. Later between 1854 and 1859, the yard concentrated on construction of Isambard Kingdom Brunel's monumental vessel *Great Eastern*, aboard which the great inventor suffered a stroke the day prior to her maiden voyage to New York from which he died a few days later. Easily the largest ship in the world at 692 feet long, *Great Eastern* had to be launched sideways into the Thames on a specially designed slipway on account of her being as long as the river was wide at that point.

The *Great Eastern* under construction at the J. Scott
Russell and Company yard circa 1857 (Alamy).

Following Scott Russell's inevitable bankruptcy in 1859, the Millwall Iron Works & Ship Building Company Ltd. was incorporated and subsequently liquidated in December 1862. In its stead, the Millwall Iron Works, Ship Building & Graving Docks Company Ltd. was floated in 1864 with a nominal capital of two million pounds in £50 shares, which investors bought up rapidly.

By the mid-1860s, the company employed between four thousand and five thousand men, making it the most ambitious yard in London. The works, divided into two primary areas, straddled the main Westferry Road. The land side comprised the heavy machinery plants, including the main forge and rolling mills for turning out angle iron and bar iron. Across the road on the riverside, linked to the forges by a horse-drawn tramway, were building slips, landing wharves, sawmills, joiners' shops,

One of the original 1864 Millwall Iron Works Ship Building & Graving Docks Company Ltd. share certificates (Author's collection).

an engine factory, foundries, sail-lofts, and a mast factory. The scale of the works was unprecedented, with the flywheel for the plate armour mill weighing over one hundred tons and having a diameter of thirty-six feet.

The Millwall Ironworks built vessels from start to finish—a pioneering concept at the time. Rather than purchasing iron from other manufacturers, both yards forged raw material on-site, giving them the ability to complete a ship without any external contribution. A contemporary observer stated that both the Thames Ironworks and Millwall Ironworks were "of infinitely greater national importance than the royal dockyards, with a production capacity for iron ships and armor greater than that of the whole of France." The RMSPC had picked the perfect yard to build their hopes for the future and oversaw construction from start to finish.

The Millwall Iron Works Ship Building & Graving Docks Company Ltd. in 1864 (Alamy).

In 1863, when *Rhone* construction started, the yard buzzed with activity where hard cockney Londoners worked in hazardous conditions producing cutting-edge vessels. *Rhone*'s design required an overall length of 326 feet with a 40-foot beam. She was to be propelled by a simple inverted five hundred horsepower, two-cylinder engine; built on-site; and fed by four square boilers supported by a condenser (which dried the steam and then condensed it to increase pressure). Further propulsion was added in the form of two masts, brig rigged, which assisted the engines when wind was available. Her interior provided 253 first-class, 30 second-class, and 30 third-class cabins, a saloon, and public areas, all lit by gullwing skylights on the deck and portholes punched through the hull. Overall, the vessel when finished weighed in at 2,738 gross tons.

The men who built *Rhone* in 1864 (Alamy).

Rhone was launched on February 11, 1865, directly in front of the Millwall Iron Works. Designers and tradesmen spent six months fitting out her luxurious passenger appointments, whilst engineers installed the engines intended to propel her around the world. At the same time, crewmen rigged and dressed her masts with sails and applied the final finishing touches. During August and September, she underwent her sea trials to the satisfaction of both her owners and insurers. On September 21, she completed the necessary running tests, having reached a top speed of fourteen knots. The following day she was officially registered and given the identification number 52792. Less than three weeks later, on October 9, 1865, amidst national interest, she left the dock at Southampton outbound to Brazil on her maiden voyage under the command of Captain Robert Woodward, a young captain at forty from Ramsgate in Kent. A fortnight later, at a meeting of the proprietors of the RMSPC, the company's chairman, Captain Charles Mangles, reported to his shareholders:

> The *Rhone* was dispatched from Southampton with the mails for Brazil on the 9th of October last. In fitting out this vessel, the comfort of passengers has been studied in every respect and very flattering opinions have already reached the directors regarding her. Now to prove that we have success, because it is the Post Office we are under and therefore it is to them we look, the directors have received a letter from the Post Office in which the following is an extract;
>
> Lord Stanley of Alderhay desires me at the same time to request that you will inform the directors that the purveying offices report that the satisfactory manner in which the *Rhone* has been built, fitted and equipped, as compared with mercantile steamers generally, reflects much credit on her builders, and also on the Royal Mail Company's assessors who superintended the construction of the vessel. I am also to add that his Lordship has sent this report with much pleasure.

Mangles went on to reflect, "I think this is very valuable and we must still study to be in a position that at the end of the contract, they cannot replace us. We must be so good that nothing can touch us."

Just months later, in January 1866, during her return voyage to Southampton from Brazil, *Rhone* was caught by a heavy storm in the Bay of Biscay during which the steamship *London*, bound for Melbourne from Gravesend, foundered with the loss of 220 lives. *Rhone*'s survival added further to her public notoriety, encouraging more customers to book passage aboard her.

The loss of the steamship *London* in 1866 (Alamy).

Having completed eight voyages on the Brazil route, the company decided to transfer *Rhone* to the West India service, which was approved on the May 16, 1867. She began her last voyage to Brazil on January 7, finally arriving back home in Southampton on Tuesday, March 5. Twelve days later, on March 17, she began her new route to the Caribbean. Sometime in August 1867, Robert Woodward left *Rhone*, and Robert Frederick Woolley, who had specifically expressed a wish to command the vessel, became her new captain.

Woolley came from Sutton-in-Ashfield in Nottinghamshire, then a busy landlocked colliery town. His rural upbringing in a mining environment some fifty-seven miles from the nearest sea should have dictated a future toiling in the dark coal pits surrounding his home, but like his brother John James Woolley, who worked for the Peninsula and Orient Shipping Company, Frederick (which he preferred to be called) pursued a life at sea that he began at an early age. He started his career with the RMSPC in January 1842 as a second officer aboard the *Dee* and was quickly promoted to first officer within a few months. Six years later, in April 1848, a senior officer commented that Woolley was "an active, good officer, highly to be recommended to command." His navigational skills, which were considered to be exceptional, coupled with his friendly and polite demeanour towards passengers, brought him to the attention of his superiors, who appointed him captain in late 1848. He had, however, commanded ships from as early as 1842 when he skippered the schooner *Lee* from Havana to Honduras for three voyages. He married a Miss Stevens who, before she died early into their marriage, produced a baby boy whom Woolley fully intended to follow in his footsteps and go to sea. Woolley joined the *Rhone* having left the *Atrato* and was accompanied by his friend and colleague, John Moorish, a thirty-four-year-old from Exeter who came aboard as purser.

The only known photograph of RMS *Rhone* afloat,
circa 1866 (Hampshire Records Office).

On October 2, 1867, the *Rhone* left Southampton for the Caribbean under the command of her new captain who, on their first night at sea, was absorbed with the logistical paperwork inherent to his position. An interesting document surviving from that night lists the changes in the ship's crew and must have been deposited onshore at the company's offices in the West Indies. According to the document, four men, Daniel Gibon, Samuel Bone, Thomas Butter, and James Clark, all missed the voyage for various reasons—Gibon by mutual consent whilst Bone is just recorded as having "Not joined." Butter and Clarke, however, are listed as having "Run," whether by pure chance or premonition. Four men are listed as having joined the ship, including Thomas Bushnell, George Barnett, William Aldred, and Samuel McCain. Only one would survive.

CHAPTER 4

"This Fairy Group of Islands"

HAVING SUCCESSFULLY COMPLETED the first leg of her voyage, *Rhone* was anchored outside Great Harbour, Peter Island (amongst the British occupied Virgin Islands) on October 29, 1867, undergoing repairs in order to pick up the mail from St. Thomas in the adjacent Danish Virgin Islands the following day before her return to Southampton. Her habitual port of call, where she normally refuelled with coal and picked up homeward-bound passengers to England, had been St. Thomas; however, prior to his arrival, Captain Woolley had met his former ship, the *Atrato*, twelve miles outside of the Virgin Islands archipelago and had been warned by her captain that yellow fever was rampant in St. Thomas. Woolley consequently decided to anchor off of Peter Island in accordance with the company's policy. Thus, he avoided a potentially fatal embarkation port for Royal Mail Steam Packet Company passengers. During a meeting held in October 1867, just four days before the fateful storm, Captain Charles Mangels, chairman of the RMSPC, in a report to his shareholders, stated:

> Most of the shareholders know that the outward bound ships went to St. Thomas, and from there were dispersed the whole of the inter-colonial ships. It became necessary from the circumstances of the government, that we should do all in our power to allocate and prevent as far as possible, so sad an occurrence as the loss of life by Yellow fever in our ships. Under the circumstances, the island of Peter, it is one of the Virgin Islands about 24 miles from St. Thomas, was selected as we believe it free from fever for our ships.

Yellow fever, also known as yellow jack, is a tropical disease that modern science believes originated in East or Central Africa from where it spread across the vast continent. Although both humans and primates are hosts to the disease, it is spread by the mosquito *Aedes aegypti* during its never ending quest for blood, a necessary ingredient for the insect's reproductive cycle. Once an individual or primate is bitten by an infected mosquito, they become infected and transmit the virus to any other mosquito that subsequently bites them, transforming that insect into a carrier and thus perpetuating the transmission cycle.

Following an incubation period of approximately three to six days, a tri-phase sequence commences beginning with a high fever and then chills, accompanied by severe back pains, headaches, nausea, vomiting, and fatigue. The second phase is in itself particularly cruel as it involves a period of remission that can lead patients into a false sense of security believing that their suffering has finished, which for most individuals is correct. For the unlucky 15 percent, however, a third phase evolves that is usually fatal. This is characterised by jaundice, which causes yellowing of the skin (hence the name), hepatitis, internal haemorrhaging, and vomiting. Ultimately, the victim falls into a state of irreversible shock, encouraging a multisystem organ failure that leads to death.

Medical historians generally concur that, like other African maladies, yellow fever found its way into the Western Hemisphere via the Atlantic slave trade, making a dramatic pan-Caribbean debut in 1648. Barbados, the most easterly of the islands, was affected by this particular epidemic as was the Yucatan Peninsula in Central America where the indigenous Maya people referred to the unknown entity as *xekik* (black vomit).

The disease made another vivid appearance in 1793 when refugees escaping from the revolution in Saint-Domingue (modern-day Haiti) arrived in Philadelphia, bringing the virus with them. Then the capital of the United States, Philadelphia lost more than four thousand people to the contagion, encouraging a mass evacuation that included the President George Washington and his government. Nineteen years later, in an attempt to recover Saint-Domingue from the rebel slaves, Napoleon Bonaparte dispatched an army of forty thousand troops to the island, which returned a year later with just one-third of the original complement, the rest having been decimated by yellow fever.

Enclosed military barracks provided an ideal breeding ground for the disease due to the large density of individuals in one confined area. Between 1793 and 1802, it is estimated that some forty-five thousand British soldiers met their end in the West Indies, including fifteen hundred officers, primarily due to yellow fever. Of the twenty-three thousand British paid troops who invaded Saint-Domingue during the revolutionary struggle, three out of five died from either yellow fever or malaria. The mortality rate for newly arrived military personal with little tolerance for tropical ailments was greater than that for the established Creole Caucasians in the region, who had somewhat acclimatised to the alien environment. During 1796, some 41 percent of fresh recruits arriving in the Caribbean region were dead within the first year. Far more British troops stationed in the West Indies died from yellow fever than from any of the contested military campaigns.

The port of Charlotte Amalie at St. Thomas in many ways resembled a military barracks on the basis that a disproportionate amount of people were confined in a very small area that with time had turned into an extremely unhealthy environment. A passenger travelling on a Royal Mail Steamer described the situation during a visit in the 1860s:

> In harbour in St. Thomas the air is often so offensive that one is forced to close the port and rather have no fresh air at all than breathe an atmosphere so villainous; the cause of this is that the harbour is tideless, and the water nearly quite stagnant, so that dead animals and garbage of all kinds thrown overboard from the ships frequently float around them for hours, and under the rays of such a sun emit a stench more easily to be imagined than described. Then the sewerage of the town inhabited by eight to ten thousand people is carried into the harbour by three of four

small streams (or rather open sewers), which deposits their filth on the shore of this stagnant pool where it lies festering from year to year, or until providence send a tornado or hurricane to clear away the filthy accumulation. Can anyone wonder that the crews of ships, sweltering for weeks in such a spot should suffer frightfully from Yellow fever.

The harbour of St. Thomas *circa* 1860s (Alamy).

In order to avoid the potential loss of passengers whilst at anchor in Charlotte Amalie, the board of the RMSPC had chosen Peter Island as a safe quarantine from where their ships could be loaded with coal. Peter Island or St. Peters Island (named after the beatified disciple) lies just 4.5 miles from Tortola. The largest bay on the leeward side of Peter Island, Great Harbour, had been chosen by the RMSPC as a temporary base where passengers could be transferred from St. Thomas, and the company's ships could be refuelled without fear of contagious infection. The small local population on the island was centred around a Methodist church between Great Harbour and Sprat Bay, where in 1867, coal had been deposited for the use of RMSPC vessels. Normally, company ships would tie up alongside the West India dock in Charlotte Amalie, St. Thomas, where locals would carry coal from the docks onto ships in baskets, filling the hungry bunkers beneath. This employment paid ready cash to the recently emancipated population and was a popular form of employment for young women known as the Black Diamonds. Regular procedure had been disrupted by Yellow fever though, and it was for this reason that *Rhone* was to be refuelled by small local sloops laden with coal from Peter Island, which provided an idyllic backdrop compared to the hustle and bustle of St. Thomas. Mr. A. W. Nesbit, a passenger from a previous voyage aboard *Rhone*, in describing the scene after the disaster, wrote:

> Often have I, from the deck of the very ship that has now gone down, looked upon this fairy group of islands, where nature has her full away, where the eye rests on all sides on the most perfect harmony of color, and where the intensity of the tropical heat is tempered by a gentle breeze. I sat there, little thinking, that below me was the future grave of my companions, and that those smiling waters were so soon to engulf the noble vessel on which I stood, and to make the name of St. Peters Island so sadly famous.

At 8:30 a.m. aboard *Rhone*, fireman David Rees and the rest of his crew were ordered below to light three fires in each boiler to get up steam. In what can only be described as a verbal oxymoron, the job of a fireman aboard steamships consisted of nurturing fires rather than extinguishing them like their terrestrial namesakes. Within the hierarchy of the engine room, theirs was one of the lowest ranked positions, second only to the trimmers who served them with fuel. The two groups together formed what was known as the Black Gang, a reference to their rarely

Fireman stoking a ship's boiler (Alamy).

bathed, coal-smothered bodies. Deep inside the bowels of the ship, massive bunkers carried tons of coal to be transferred into energy. The burning coal was used to heat the water in the boilers creating steam which, when introduced into the cylinders, generated pressure that subsequently turned the propeller shaft. Trimmers would position the coal next to the bunker door, and the firemen would collect the fossilised wood to stoke the boilers. They would also make sure that the bunkers were trimmed evenly with coal to avoid instability and the potential for capsizing in heavy seas.

Apart from just shovelling fuel into the boilers, a fireman also maintained the most efficient flame possible, which required more skill than just adding coal. Of constant concern to the firemen was the buildup of clinkers, or fused lumps of non-combustible coal, which could prevent sufficient air reaching the rest of the firebed. Firemen had a variety of different tools at their disposal for dealing with this issue. They used pricker bars to rake the gratings free of any ash or clinkers obstructing the airflow, devils claws to remove the offending clinkers, and firing hoes to gently rake the tops of the fires and spread the burning material evenly in order to create the ideal fire—bright light yellow all over. Once the first fires had been successfully ignited, the question of pressure became of paramount importance in order to determine the ability of a stationary ship to move. Higher pressure provided more controllability, and by 9:00 a.m. aboard

Rhone, instructions had been passed down to ignite the remaining boiler fires bringing the pressure up to fifteen pounds.

By this time, *Rhone*'s barometer stood at thirty inches with winds blowing from the south-southeast. Most of the passengers would have been on deck in an effort to escape the claustrophobic iron hull which, even with the butterfly hatches and portholes open, rapidly heated up in the morning sun. The *Conway*, a veteran of the West India station, was tied alongside *Rhone* in the calm lee of the island, which had in the past accommodated six RMSPC vessels rafted up together. In accordance with the strict class divisions of the day, first-class passengers had the freedom of the ship's stern half whilst second-class passengers were confined forward of the funnel to the most uncomfortable area when underway. Even the ship's crockery reflected these boundaries with first-class plates sporting the company coat of arms whilst second-class plates clearly stated by whom they were meant to be used.

The *Rhone* and *Conway* rafted alongside each other
prior to the storm (George Wilkinson).

Although passengers were oblivious to the impending danger whilst indifferently watching cargo and stores being transferred from *Conway* to *Rhone*, Virgin Islanders would have recognised the warning signs of an impending tempest beginning with a storm swell followed by an abnormal rise in the tide. High clouds then shifted outwards in all directions away from the storm, leaving tufted cirrus clouds remaining as an ominous precursor. The complete lack of any breeze provided a final harbinger as the looming hurricane sucked the immediate weather into its spiralling embrace.

By 9:30 a.m., the barometer aboard *Rhone* had fallen to 29.39 inches, and Captain Woolley, who was on deck with Captain Hammock of *Conway*, stated that "he did not like the look of the weather, and as the hurricane season was over, it must be a Norther brewing, and that he should shift to an anchorage under the Northern Islands." Consequently, it was decided to transfer passengers from *Conway* to *Rhone* in the belief that they would be safer on the larger, more modern vessel. Three weeks later, the *Hampshire Chronicle* referred to one of those passengers, who was overheard by a subsequent survivor saying to his wife as they boarded *Rhone*, "Thank God we are safe here." Minutes later, as the sea became choppier, the gangway had to be withdrawn between the two ships leaving a woman named Nurse (whose husband had died of Yellow fever in Demerara) and her two children, who had been due to return to Southampton aboard *Rhone*, stranded on *Conway* thus saving their lives.

Conversely, the chief officer of *Conway*, Mr. Fry, who had been aboard *Rhone* supervising the transfer of cargo, was unable to return to his ship before the gangway was retracted. At 11:10 a.m., with the barometer now reading 27.95 inches, *Rhone* and *Conway* separated with Captain Woolley hailing to Captain Hammock that he could not steam against such a wind and that he intended on riding out the storm at anchor. By noon, the storm was upon the Virgin Islands, and the full validity of the situation became apparent to both skippers.

The *Rhone* and *Conway* separate at the beginning of the storm (George Wilkinson).

As Captain Hammock struggled to cross the Sir Francis Drake Channel dividing Peter Island and Tortola, Captain Woolley attempted to ride out the storm at anchor. It was during this first assault by the hurricane that First Officer Dalby Topper, a thirty-five-year-old Londoner, was killed aboard *Rhone* by a falling spar.

Sometime between 12:30 p.m. and 1:00 p.m., the eye of the storm passed over Tortola, providing Captain Woolley with the option of weighing anchor and heading out into the open sea, which he decided to pursue. Unfortunately, whilst raising the anchor, one of the chain shackles became caught in the hawse pipe and parted with sixty fathoms (360 feet) of chain leaving *Rhone* adrift. With the boiler pressure standing at twenty pounds, the maximum they were designed to bear, *Rhone* headed into the Sir Francis Drake Channel at full speed. The last time anyone saw her afloat was just after 1:00 p.m., heading for the passage between

Chief Officer Dalby Topper killed by a falling spar (George Wilkinson).

Dead Man's Chest and Salt Island. Knowing that a shallow submerged plateau christened Blonde Rock lay in the middle of the gap, Captain Woolley gave the area a wide berth, bringing him closer to Salt Island.

Whilst the eye of the hurricane passed overhead, providing a brief respite for the two struggling vessels, both steamed frantically for safety before the inevitable onslaught recommenced. By 1:30 p.m., the second front began blistering through the Sir Francis Drake Channel, thrashing anything that came within its path. *Conway*, by now close to Road Harbour, was hit by a sudden gust of wind that blew in her portholes, threatening to sink her. Following a brief lull during which Captain Hammock pointed his bow to the southwest, a second gust blew away *Conway*'s main mast and funnel, leaving her to the mercy of the elements. Fortunately, the wind direction pushed the aging ship into Road Harbour where she went ashore somewhere in the vicinity of Port Purcell and was saved without loss of life. Aboard *Rhone*, however, a more dramatic scenario was beginning to unfold.

Captain Woolley was profoundly aware of the fact that his best option lay in reaching open sea where he could ride out the storm without fear of colliding into obstructions. *Rhone* had already proven her seaworthiness twenty-one months earlier in the Bay of Biscay. With the knowledge that vessels rarely founder without hitting something first, Woolley knew that he had to guide his ship out of the Sir Francis Drake Channel, which is practically a landlocked lake apart from a few narrow, hazardous gaps between the islands. Later knowledge revealed that the option to drop a second anchor had been available, but the experienced captain never considered this an alternative and instead decided to make a break, which, were it not for the timing, would have been the correct decision. Had Woolley headed for open water ten minutes earlier, he would have guided his ship past Salt Island to the safety of deep water where, like *Rhone*'s sister ship *Douro*, he could have weathered the hurricane at sea. If he had left ten minutes later, it is likely that *Rhone* would have been grounded in Lee Bay, Salt Island, with little if any loss of life and the possibility of the ship being salvaged. Fate and nature combined to provide circumstances beyond Robert Woolley's control, though, which proved fatal for the pride of the RMSPC fleet.

The *Rhone* steaming for open water (George Wilkinson).

Meanwhile, at adjacent St. Thomas in the Danish Virgin Islands, there was nothing threatening in the appearance of the morning until about 11:00 a.m. when a light drizzle began to fall and the wind blew out of the south. By 12:30 p.m., the wind was blowing more urgently out of the west, encouraging a crowd of people to gather on the wharves and shoreline of Charlotte Amalie in the misguided belief that they were about to witness a sea storm. At this time, no precautions had been taken to secure houses on St. Thomas due to the naive belief that the hurricane season was finished. By 1:15 p.m., though, the storm was passing overhead, and the ships in the harbour began dragging their anchors in a mournful procession towards the west side of the bay. Realising their mistake, the foolhardy spectators began racing for cover, but many were caught in the storm and taken out to sea, never to be seen again.

Twenty-six miles away, at approximately 1:30 p.m., *Rhone*, having cleared Blonde Rock, began rounding Salt Island beyond which was

The *Rhone* approaching Black Rock Point, Salt Island (George Wilkinson).

open water and relative safety. The second front of the hurricane was attending the islands with full force by this time, blowing freak gusts of unpredictable wind from the northwest, with visibility no more than the ship's length. Captain Woolley realised that his vessel was too close to Salt Island and consequently gave orders to turn her stern full about in order to avoid the point of Lee Bay; in doing so, this put *Rhone* beam to the wind and out of control. Immediately afterwards, the direction of the storm took a sudden change to the southeast, pushing *Rhone* towards Black Rock Point. Inevitably, as she approached the rocks, panic broke out amongst the bewildered passengers. Captain Woolley meanwhile turned to his warrant officer, Mr. Holdeman, saying, "Good Lord, is it ever possible," to which Holdeman responded, "Yes Sir, the ships ashore."

CHAPTER 5

The Sinking of RMS *Rhone*

AT OR VERY close to 2:00 p.m., *Rhone*, running at full speed, struck Black Rock Point on Salt Island amidships on her port side. The earlier dramatic course alteration combined with a sudden change in wind direction had slewed her stern around, and the last sighting of Captain Robert Woolley was at the ship's wheel with Purser John Morrish, both desperately trying to steer *Rhone*'s bow into the wind. A wave broke over the deck, throwing Woolley onto a skylight from where he was washed into the sea between the hull and the rocks. "The first striking shivered almost everything fore and aft," but *Rhone* came off, only to be pushed up again:

The *Rhone* strikes Black Rock Point at approximately 2:00 p.m. (George Wilkinson).

Twice she struck and boats and spars and sheep pens flew across the deck, then she parted amidships, the stern portion swung round and the waves rushing in between her decks, ripped them up as though with an explosion of gunpowder; the passengers who were lashed on deck being swallowed up in the chasm.

Down below, Fireman Henry Buckell remained at his post "until the chief engineer called us up from below, when the ship broke in halves, and I went up the skylight." Buckell recalled, "I saw the sea break right through her side, and when I got on deck I saw the sea come right over her. I saw many persons rushing to the fore companion, and up through the skylight onto the spar deck."

Fellow fireman David Rees gave a similar account:

> What I fancy is that when she struck first she "kind of scurged" a rock on the port side; the second time it seemed to lift her, and she went down "bump" and bumped three or four times. Of course it drove her sides in, and I believe that the rocks went up at the bottom into her boilers. Seeing the water coming into the stoke hole, I got up through the engine room ladder; all that I saw was a boiler maker in the engine room, and he went up the ladder before me. When I got on the top, the steam pipe burst and everything being covered with steam, I lost sight of all that was going on. The men in the stoke hole had no chance to come up. Two came up but they were fearfully scolded; their names were Lane and Arthur Cull. As I knew the way out as well in the dark as the light, I got hold of the handrail, and crawled out of the steam under the door. When I got out I found the forward companion covered with people. The main deck people were clinging to everything they saw. I rushed right through them onto the spar deck, where I was washed off, and overboard, and the bow of the vessel came right round to me.

Jonathan Bailey, a sixteen-year-old ship's boy, vividly described his ship's demise:

> It was only then about 2 o clock, but it was dark as any night, and the wind was the maddest that ever I see, and the hailstones came pelting down quite as big as marbles. I was below, just when she struck, but I ran up quick, and as soon as I got on deck I was carried off my legs and dashed against the rails at the side, and held there by the wind so tight that I couldn't break away. At last I managed it, and then I found that everybody was doing his best to save himself. When I say that I found it out, that isn't quite right, it wasn't a time to find things out. Along with the hail the splinters and spars were whirling about and knocking together about your ears, and the wind was roaring and people shouting and shrieking, and the surf banging against the rocks and throwing up a great sheet all white as snow and high as this house or higher.
>
> I knew a good many aboard of course, but that wasn't a time to look after 'em. You couldn't hear your own voice even though you bawled what you thought was ever so loud. I saw a man I knew very well, an' he was holding on while he slipped one of our life buoys over his shoulder. I didn't expect it, of course, but I asked in a fright to let me have the buoy. I don't suppose he heard what I said. He took no notice.
>
> 'I scrambled away to the stern which was stuck up high on the rocks, and I looked down and I thought I might jump it. It wasn't so very deep, and anyhow it was something to stand on, and it didn't so much matter if I got no worse than a sprain; so I chanced it. I had no shoes on, nor any cap. I made the jump but somehow I missed. I can't tell you how or why I missed, but I fell half into the sea, and the surf came in a minute and licked me off and carried me out.'

One of the engineers stated that there had been an explosion in the boiler room that blew out the bottom of the ship, causing it to separate.

This explanation was later supported by Purser Whitmarsh of the *Douro*, who had interviewed other survivors and surmised, "It was thought that onboard *Rhone* there were more killed than drowned, through the explosion and breaking up of the ship." It would appear, however, that the tremendous noise associated with the ship splitting apart was confused for an explosion. Another survivor stated that "the *Rhone* parted amidships, and the waves ripped up the gigantic steamer as if she were made of brown paper." Survivors concurred with the fact that the quick, catastrophic demolition of the ship was responsible for the high mortality rate. Rees stated, "My opinion is that more were killed by the knocking about of the wreck than being drowned," whilst Holdeman was convinced that he "never saw one person drowned."

The *Rhone* breaks up (George Wilkinson).

Whilst their ship sank beneath them, survivors of the initial impact frantically struggled to save themselves by clinging on to anything available. The fierce nature of the storm, combined with extensive floating wreckage created when the ship broke apart, provided a hazardous environment from which few escaped. Much to his relief, Jonathan Bailey was pulled out to sea away from the carnage. He noted:

> It was lucky that I was drifted out a bit, because it put me out of the way of the bits of wreck that closer in shore were smashing and grinding about. The wind took the lighter bits of timber and drove them against the heavy bits, and it would have been awkward to have got between the two. It made great splinters fly up as big as plates and dishes.

Josiah Metcalfe, an invalided seaman and consequently a passenger, recalled seeing a group of people on the companionway being engulfed in a moment with the exception of one boy, whom he last saw in the shrouds engulfed in prayer. Subsequently, Metcalfe was swept into the rigging, where he secured himself, then afterwards swam to the foreyard and there remained. Once the bow had slewed around from Black Rock Point, it sank intact and upright in approximately eighty feet of water with the forward mast standing proud above the surface. It was here that Metcalfe found sanctuary from the chaotic mess beneath him, only to discover that four others had got there first. One of these was Fireman David Rees who, once in the water, "saw the chief engineer, Mr. Hopper, clinging to a skylight, and was washed by him. He looked at me and I looked at him, just as men will do at such times." Hopper would not survive, but Rees "clung to the foretopsail yard, from where I stopped until half past eight next morning."

Jonathan Bailey, who minutes earlier had been swept out to sea away from the rocks, desperately looked around for some form of buoyancy.

> There was plenty to lay hold of to keep you afloat, plenty on the water, pitching and tossing, and plenty more climbing down from the ship, that was being blown to bits. I don't know exactly

Crew members cling to the fore top yard (George Wilkinson).

what it was that I got hold of. It was wood, and large enough to keep me floating anyhow. But it was all a job to keep a hold on it, Sir, I can tell you, the wind was snatching and whirling things in such a way. Well, I stuck to my stick, and was washed out and in, out and in, every time thinking when I was washed in that now I should be able to reach the rock again and scramble up it, and each time being swept back when it seemed that I had only to put out my hand. I didn't like to put out my hand too soon; I should have lost my float very likely if I had done so.

Some crew members and one passenger managed to make it ashore on Salt Island. There, they sought help at the local settlement some distance away from the wreck site, across the salt pond. The passenger, an Italian whose name is not recorded but who resided in Pennsylvania, recalled that when he found himself close to shore:

He and others were washed up on the island and were unable to walk on the rocks in consequence of what seaman term "pears," which pricked their feet severely; and he was compelled to tear up his shirt and bind the pieces around his naked feet in order to move about.

Meanwhile, as other survivors were swept out to sea and the storm gradually diminished, the bodies of those who had gone down with the ship began to surface and mix with the corpses already drifting amongst the flotsam. It was around this time that the first sharks arrived on the scene.

The presence of a variety of sharks in the Virgin Islands provides a necessary series of apex predators in a remarkably diverse marine ecosystem, but it is extremely rare for humans to encounter them. Humankind's morbid fascination with these large marine *selachii* is probably unparalleled by any other creature on Earth. Having begun their evolution during the Devonian era, some four hundred million years ago, they reached an apogee during the Cenozoic era, twenty-eight million years ago, with the appearance of the *meglodon*, which reached between forty and sixty feet in length and is thought to have looked similar to the great white sharks living today but much stockier. This horrific predator became extinct during the Pleistocene era some 1.5 million years ago and was arguably the most formidable carnivore ever to have existed.

Scientists generally agree that most species of sharks have remained unchanged for millions of years, providing a testimony to their genetic efficiency. There are over four hundred varieties of sharks with new species still being discovered occasionally. Some are completely harmless, whilst others, including the great white shark (*Carcharodon carcharias*), bull shark (*Carcharhinus leucas*), tiger shark (*Galeocerdo cuvier*), and oceanic whitetip shark (*Carcharhinus longimanus*), are known to be anthropophagus—consumers of human flesh. One of the earliest written descriptions of sharks was provided by the second-century Greek poet

Oppian, who in his *Halieutica* described how they "raved for food with increasing frenzy, being always hungered and never abating the gluttony of their terrible maw; for what food shall be sufficient to fill the void of their belly or enough to satisfy and give respite to their insatiable jaws?"

On the other side of the world, where ships grew more sophisticated, prompting greater international trade, travellers' accounts reported on shark sightings to the Europeans who immediately categorised them as heinous villains.

James Thomson's 1783 poem "Summer" epitomised the accepted contemporary profile for sharks.

> Here dwells the direful shark. Lur'd by the scent
> Of streaming crouds, of rank disease, & death,
> Behold! He rushing cuts the briny flood,
> Swift as the gale can bear the ship along;
> And, from the partners of that cruel trade,
> Which spoils unhappy Guinea of her sons,
> Demands his share of prey; demands themselves.
> The stormy fates descend: one death involves
> Tyrants and slaves; when strait, their mangled limbs
> Crashing at once, he dyes the purple seas
> With gore, and riots in the vengeant meal.

Mariners, due the nature of their employment, inevitably encountered the large predators that habitually followed vessels in the hope of obtaining easy food. The zoologist Thomas Pennant, in his *Treasury of Natural History*, describes:

> They devour with indiscriminating voracity almost every animal substance, whether living or dead. They often follow vessels for the sake of picking up any offal that may be thrown overboard, and, in hot climates especially, man himself becomes a victim to their rapacity. No fish can swim with such velocity as the shark,

nor is any so constantly engaged in that exercise; he outstrips the swiftest ships, and plays round them, without exhibiting a symptom of strong exertion or uneasy apprehension; and the depredations he commits on the other inhabitants of the deep are truly formidable.

Shipwrecks inevitably encouraged sharks to gather and feed on the living (and dead) who found themselves in open water unprotected. A famous example of this, christened the Birkenhead Drill, encouraged the evacuation procedure of women and children embarking upon lifeboats ahead of men. The name came from HMS *Birkenhead*, a ship that struck an uncharted submerged rock near Algoa Bay in South Africa during the Kaffir War.

Immediately following impact, her captain ordered an anchor to be dropped and then attempted to draw the ship off the rocks, which allowed water to flood through a gaping hole in the side of the vessel, resulting in the death of one hundred soldiers in their berths. The remaining officers and men mustered on the deck where they watched the women and children lowered into the water aboard the ship's cutter. Ten minutes later, the ship struck the rock a second time tearing apart the hull and splitting the ship into two just aft of the mainmast. An officer writing to his father recalled the event in some detail.

> I remained on the wreck until she went down; the suction took me down some way, and a man got hold of my leg, but I managed to kick him off and came up and struck out for some pieces of wood that were on the water and started for land, about two miles off. I was in the water about five hours, as the shore was so rocky and the surf ran so high that a great many were lost trying to land. Nearly all those that took to the water without their clothes on were taken by sharks; hundreds of them were all round us, and I saw men taken by them close to me, but as I was dressed (having on a flannel shirt and trousers) they preferred

the others. I was not in the least hurt, and am happy to say, kept my head clear; most of the officers lost their lives from losing their presence of mind and trying to take money with them, and from not throwing off their coats.

Of the 643 people onboard at the time of the sinking, only 193 survived to tell the authorities what had transpired. The majority of casualties were taken by sharks who had been attracted to the commotion on what was otherwise a calm and clear night.

Twenty-five years later, a journalist writing about the *Rhone* disaster observed, "One of the frightful accompaniments of the fearful and numerous wrecks and the agonizing state of the survivors, whether for a time or an ultimate deliverance, was the presence of sharks in every direction." For the five crew members precariously perched on the foretop yard, just one hundred feet from the shore, the feeding frenzy of sharks taking place in the water beneath them negated the option of swimming the short distance to Salt Island. Josiah Metcalfe remembered afterwards, "During this time he was within a comparatively short distance from the rocks, but dared not venture to swim towards them from the certainty of a horrible death, wither from the sharks or from being dashed to pieces on the rocks."

David Rees likewise reported, "I am a good swimmer, but the next morning the sharks were lying around us like little fish, and therefore twas useless to think of swimming in order to get relieved and picked up."

As well as feeding on corpses, the sharks attacked survivors, which Jonathan Bailey witnessed firsthand.

> I caught sight of a man keeping up with a buoy. I knew who it was at once. It was the same man that I spoke to when he was putting on the buoy just before we broke up. I don't think that he saw me, but seeing nobody else about, it was like company for me to keep sight of him, and so I did. Well, presently, all of sudden, I

saw him throw up his arms over his head, and down he slipped out of the buoy like a bolt out of a socket. Well, you see, Sir, when you ask me how to account for it, that is more than I can tell you exactly, so as to make sure, you know; but the sharks in them waters are something more than ordinary. He was nipped of at the legs, that's how I reckon it up.

With daylight fading, those remaining alive in the water drifted helplessly on whatever became buoyantly available once *Rhone* had come to rest on the seabed beneath them. Eight men drifted down the Sir Francis Drake Channel on an upturned lifeboat, whilst two men, Francis Brewer and Frederick Pearse (just sixteen at the time), clung desperately to a floating plank that carried them to Beef Island. Likewise, John Palmer and Samuel McCane, both able seaman aboard the ill-fated vessel, drifted to Beef Island in life rings that they later complained had after a few hours of soaking in the water became soddened, and like to weigh them down rather than bear them up. Five others, George Holdeman, Henry Buckle, John Jones, Thomas Ingram, and Frederick Hamford (Hanaford), all managed to climb into a hammock bin, an oblong wooden box used to stow crew member's sleeping cradles when their occupants were on duty. This unseaworthy makeshift boat they had scrambled into was made more precarious by a hole in the side that waterlogged the interior until the boatswain's mate, Charles Moody, appeared clasping a spar he had found, "and seeing how likely they were to capsize, he poked one end of the spar he was floating on into the hole stove in the side of the bin, and holding onto it with one arm, swam with the other and so he bought them nigh to land."

Meanwhile, young Jonathan Bailey had recovered the recently vacated lifebuoy and began floating towards Beef Island in an exhausted state. He eventually fell asleep, wrapping his arms through the cords of the buoy, when suddenly he felt something knock against his legs.

> I woke up again, feeling a rasping against my leg, and there and then the thought of sharks came into my head, and I roused up pretty quick. But it wasn't a shark. I had drifted to the shore, and was stranded on a sandbank. I wasn't hurt a bit, and not even bruised, to speak of, but I was very cold and empty feeling, and my teeth all of a chatter, As far as I reckon, keeping account of the hours afterwards, it was about one o clock in the morning when I found myself stranded, and no it wasn't so dark but that I could make out the shore. Between the shore and the sand bank was about three quarters of a mile, and knowing that it was no use staying where I was, I went in, with my life buoy still on, and swum it.

Once ashore, Bailey curled up in his lifebuoy and closed his eyes to a day that had seen one of the most powerful Caribbean storms in recorded history. In the short space of approximately five hours, what today would be considered a category-three hurricane had swept through the Virgin Islands directly overhead, creating absolute destruction on a scale not witnessed since September 1819, when a similar storm ruined the sugar economy in the region. By nightfall, hundreds of lives had been lost and dozens of ships foundered, including the *Rhone*, pride of the RMSPC fleet, now shattered to pieces and a complete loss. A subsequent narrator of the incident observed, "The wreck of the *Rhone* may be considered in some respects the most disastrous of any that has befallen the Royal Mail Company's ships."

CHAPTER 6

Aftermath

THE FOLLOWING MORNING, daylight revealed universal carnage in the bay of Charlotte Amalie, St. Thomas, where just twenty-four hours earlier, dozens of vessels manned by hundreds of seaman had idled at anchor oblivious to the impending disaster. The bodies of crew members littered the shoreline while their ships rested on the seabed, some on top of one another. The RMS *Wye* had sunk at Buck Island with the loss of sixty-five people, whilst the RMS *Tyne* was dismasted, and the RMS *Derwent* went ashore. The storm wrecked or seriously damaged some seventy-five vessels, with the loss of approximately five hundred lives. In describing the scene, Captain Vesey of HMS *Doris*, who arrived at St. Thomas on the morning of November 3, stated:

> All the islands appeared as if a fire had passed over them. The town of St. Thomas looks exactly as if an explosion had taken place, roofs, doors, and windows having been blown away, and the streets are filled with tiles, trees and rubbish. The harbor is full of wrecks and the dock, which some time ago went down suddenly, has had nine vessels against it and several are sunk at one end of it at the present moment. The West India and Pacific Mail Company's steamer *Columbian* is one of them with £400,000 of cargo on board. The great ship *British Empire* (formerly the *Demerara* steamer) is one and outside her are, I believe, several other vessels. The Royal Mail Steamer *Derwent* is in eight feet of water with an American ship alongside her. Inside them

are the *Robert Todd* Steamer (La Guayra packet) and a Spanish steamer, the latter quite destroyed; another Spanish steamer is near wrecked.

Damaged ships in St. Thomas Harbour, October 30, 1867 (Alamy).

Vesey subsequently received an urgent request from Sir Arthur Rumbold, president of the British Virgin Islands, requiring immediate assistance. He arrived at Tortola and wrote the following report:

> Immediately on anchoring I communicated with the president, who informed me that the total population of the islands was about 7000. That at Road Town, Tortola, there were only about 18 houses left, the gaol, pier, poorhouse, and hospital destroyed. At Kingstown only four of five houses are left; at West End, four or five out of eighty houses are left. Every church and chapel in the island has been unroofed, and all the sugar works on the estates are gone. The canes also have been destroyed and in fact, the islands have been swept clean. In the town, 23 lives lost, at Kingstown, 5, Peters Island, 2 and Spanishtown, 6. Sombrero has not been struck and Anegada has escaped, but I hear there are two wrecks on it.

Meanwhile on Beef Island, survivors from the *Rhone* were staggering barefoot through the thorny bush, attempting to make contact with anyone who could help them. Jonathan Bailey, who had made it ashore in the early hours of the morning, had no idea where he was, and in a bewildered state, started searching for signs of life.

He considered his new surroundings.

A very wild sort of place, covered all towards the sea with a thorny sort of grass which pricks like pins. I didn't have any shoes on, so that I couldn't walk about very fast; besides, I didn't know where I was walking too.

I limped about for something like an hour and a half, till it seemed to grow a little lighter, and presently I spied two men looking about 'em. They were men of the *Rhone* both. Brewer the yeoman, and Fred Pearse, engineers servant. They had both been on the island a couple of hours, they told me. Pearse had got a finger smashed. Brewer had no shoes on and Fred Pearse had one boot on. They had both got to the shore on one plank. We were very glad to meet and thought that now there would be a chance to meet some more of our fellows.

We made the best way we could over the prickles until day, when we came upon a local and two boys. They had seen something of the wrecks, and were going down to the beach to see what they could pick up. They had nothing to give us, nor could they tell us where we could get a drink of water. The local told us that he had passed and spoke to two other white men on the road and that they were not far ahead. We hurried after them and overtook them. They were both able seaman of the *Rhone*, John Palmer and Samuel McCane. Neither had shoes and McCane's clothes had been washed off him all but his smock.

Now there were five of us, and we walked along until we saw smoke, and presently came on another local who had made a fire in a bush. He told us what he was doing, but I forgot. It was something that required a heat, and his boat had been smashed up in the hurricane, and he had been cast ashore, and didn't know what to be at any more than we did. He knew whereabouts the governor's house was, though, and we persuaded him to take a message there, while we minded his fire. We should have gone ourselves only that the way was all across the prickles, and our feet were in a bad state with the walking we had already done. It was two miles to the governor's house.

It wasn't far down to the beach from where we were, so while the local was gone up to the house we went down there on the chance of picking up something to eat. We were lucky. Some of the ships wrecked had pineapples and oranges amongst their cargoes, and a goodish many of these were strewn about. They were none the better for being soaked in the sea, but we were not very particular and made a grandish breakfast out of 'em. Likewise we found two hammock cloths, which we wrung out and spread to dry in the sun to make a kind of thing to keep the sun from scorching. It wouldn't have felt so hot yet awhile, only we had been so long soaking in the salt water that our flesh was tender. If ever you have to try it, Sir, you will find out what a difference it makes.

Eventually, a Tortola mail boat picked up *Rhone*'s survivors on Beef Island and took them to Salt Island where the five men who had taken refuge on the foretop yard the day before were waiting, having been rescued that morning from their perch by a small fishing punt. Another ten men were rescued from the Sir Francis Drake Channel where they had clung to an upturned lifeboat throughout the night.

The bodies of those washed ashore were buried in a small graveyard towards the west side of Lee Bay. Amongst those interred were Samuel Daly, a twenty-seven-year-old barman, and Dalby Topper, the chief officer who had been killed when the hurricane first struck. Prior to Topper's burial, George Holdeman removed his signet ring in order to return it to his family. A number of other bodies were also buried on Salt Island, but their identities remain unknown, and they were described as being unrecognisable. Some bodies washed ashore at Tortola and were buried at a site that is now a public cemetery towards the west end of the island. The exact number of crew members and officers who died when *Rhone* sank is recorded differently by various reports at around 124, with just 22 survivors. There is confusion as to how many passengers died on the basis that some had abandoned *Conway* on the morning of the storm and had not been accurately entered into *Rhone*'s manifest.

Even though the RMSPC issued a reward for the recovery and delivery of Robert Woolley's body to the RMSPC headquarters at St. Thomas, all that was found of him were his coat sleeves, presumably identifiable by his four captain stripes. Like most of the people who perished aboard *Rhone*, he had likely died when the ship hit Black Rock Point and ripped apart and then later received attention from the numerous sharks that subsequently congregated at the wreck site. James D. Lamb, Her Britannic Majesty's consul at Saint Thomas, in a letter to the *Times*, wrote:

> The terrible fate of Captain Woolley, a gentleman esteemed by everyone that knew him both for his kind, sterling character and for his great skill and experience as a commander, is severely felt among his numerous friends. Every act of his was guided by a sense of duty and a keen appreciation of the heavy responsibilities of his position and, by his untimely death, the Royal Mail Company have lost the services of a valuable officer, and a deep sorrow is bought upon an aged and fond parent.

A letter written afterwards by one of Woolley's siblings to a friend lamented:

> It is indeed true that our darling Fred has been taken from us, taken from us in a way we cannot realize. It seems impossible

that we shall never see his dear, sweet face, again: it is so awful, so sudden, and so unexpected. A few days only before we heard the terrible news we had a letter from him, saying he had had such a splendid voyage, and was looking forward to his return home with so much pleasure, hoping we might all meet again in health and strength. How little we can forsee. Our only consolation is that he was best fitted to go; and there is the blessing left of feeling that he had lived a life of preparation for this hasty and awful summons. It was a shock, as you may imagine, to my poor, dear mother; but she at times forgets, and at other times seems to realize it all, bearing up with the thought that she will soon go to him. [Mrs. Woolley was over eighty years old at the time and a widow.]

One thing of those who knew him will be sung that thoughts of his own personal safety would never tempt him to leave the vessel, so long as there was a single human being on board.

Curiously, on a previous voyage whilst socializing with passengers, Captain Woolley had said to a Mr. Frederick Clifford (who later recalled the conversation), "If ever this ship be lost, I hope I shall go down with it."

Once the remaining survivors had been picked up and the bodies of those recovered buried, the dismasted RMS *Tyne* shipped the bewildered mariners to St. Thomas where they boarded *Rhone*'s sister ship *Douro* in preparation for the return journey to Southampton. Naturally, sailors from the *Douro* were familiar with many of the missing crew members and "eager were the questions asked of the seaman rescued from *Rhone*, who sadly paced the deck, walking like men in a dream, so awful had been the shock of what they had gone through."

When the hurricane struck, *Douro* had been some 230 miles away, steaming towards the Virgin Islands, and experienced heavy seas and gale-force winds. As she approached her destination, there was little to indicate the scale of what had occurred the previous day, but the crew noticed abnormal changes. An officer from the ship recorded:

The existence of a strong and unexpected current bearing away to the south had been detected, and less watchful eyes than those of the commander and the officers of the ship had noticed a loss of brilliancy in the water, which from the deep Atlantic blue had changed to a dead black. Someone, too, thought he made out a wreck under the land not far away; but, with the bright sun over and the smooth water below, the idea that it could be recent occurred to no one; and yet that mast with its tattered sails, was all that remained above the water of the ill fated *Rhone*.

The *Rhone*'s forward mast the following morning (George Wilkinson).

Captain Vesey, aboard HMS *Doris*, had received an urgent communication to proceed to the Virgin Islands from where he wrote a report the day he arrived:

In rounding Salt Island, I passed the wreck of the R. M. S. Packet *Rhone*. Her poop rail was close to a large boulder on the west point, but the hull was standing under water. The foremast was standing, but the vessel herself was broken in two and her head slewed to the North. Fifty yards either way would have put her into a sandy bay.

At St. Thomas, the superintendent of the RMSPC operations there, Mr. J. B. Cameron, tried to make some sense out of the chaos created by the storm. Not only had the company lost two ships with an appalling loss of life, with an additional two ships badly damaged, but the storm had levelled their headquarters, warehouses, and wharves, creating an administrative and logistical nightmare. Dazed survivors whose houses had been completely destroyed along with their belongings filled the port town of Charlotte Amalie.

A further threat from disease became apparent when the bodies of those killed when vessels sank began washing up along the shoreline in a decomposed state. A witness describing the scene wrote:

> At various points along the beach, crowds of people were collected and from each was carried away with dreadful regularity strings of rough coffins containing the dead which the sea had given up. By four o clock on the afternoon of the 30th, 292 bodies had been washed on shore and buried, and the systematic way that people worked under the guidance of the police was a sad proof of the practice they had had by that time at this mournful occupation.

Surviving crew members from wrecked British vessels working alongside the local Danish garrison managed to inter some two hundred corpses, but this represented less than half of the butcher's bill for the storm. The "harbour was specked here and there with floating human carcasses and relatives and friends in boats picking up the dead and screaming with grief and horror as the bodies were identified." On Buck Island, fifty cadavers lay together in a small bay but could not be approached for sanitary reasons, whilst scores of others were trapped inside the wrecked vessels. In an effort to retrieve these remains, Captain Vesey loaned the governor of St. Thomas some hard-hat diving apparatus, but more was needed.

> The most shocking sights were reserved for the 31st [October]. On that morning more than 100 dead bodies in an advanced state of putrefaction were seen lining the entire western beach of the harbour. This day, identification was impossible, except from clothes or a ring. The human face, distorted, swollen and decayed, presented the most hideous spectacle imaginable. The sight was indescribably distressing and deeply humiliating to the pride of man. Pitch in barrels was kept burning to dissipate the foetid effluvia, and although the corpses were hurried away to the cemetery as quickly as possible, yet many had to lie for hours on the beach, baking in the sun, and others at the surface, soaking in the water awaiting sepulcher.

In total, Vesey reckoned that some seventy-five vessels had been damaged or wrecked and the town destroyed at an estimated cost of between 1.5 and 2 million dollars. The loss of life during the catastrophe, including those still trapped in the wrecks, was around five hundred, but this later rose to over six hundred. An officer from the *Douro* observed, "A bombarded town could not have presented a worse picture of ruin and desolation."

Today, storms are carefully tracked, subsequently named, and their strength gauged according to a category of one to five based on the Saffir–Simpson hurricane wind scale. In 1867, no such classification existed, but data for the period records that the storm, which later became known as the San Narciso hurricane, was the ninth of the season, and when it reached the Virgin Islands had sustained winds of between 120 and 130 miles per hour, making it a category-three major hurricane. An idea of the storm's intensity can be measured by the fact that a fourteen-knot steamer in the harbour of St. Thomas running at full speed ahead was still pushed back and wrecked on the shore whilst every vessel that attempted to make it out to sea was lost. After devastating the Virgin Islands, the hurricane went on to wreak havoc in Puerto Rico, just sixty miles away, where the devastation was so complete the island fell into economic turmoil, prompting a revolt against Spanish colonialism a year later that was christened the Grito Del Lares (Cry of Lares).

Amid this scene of desolation, *Douro* refilled her bunkers and began her lugubrious journey back to Southampton on November 5. After a voyage of sixteen days, she sailed into Plymouth where her captain communicated news of his arrival to the company offices in Southampton. Immediately, the RMSPC hoisted the company flag at their headquarters in Canute Road to alert the town's residents of the steamer's return. News had reached Southampton via telegraph that a violent storm had occurred in the West Indies, but no specific details had been transmitted. *Douro* subsequently anchored off of Netley Hospital near Southampton at 10:30 p.m., from where a clearer picture of the disaster was painted for the anxious families and relatives of RMSPC crew members. The following morning, a survivor list was posted outside the offices on Canute Road where people had nervously gathered.

> Copies of the lists of the saved were prepared and exhibited in various other places, and in every instance they were scanned over by hundreds of anxious eyes to ascertain whether the name of a husband, a son, a brother, or a friend was enrolled among those who had happily escaped with their lives. The dejected countenances unmistakably proclaimed that the large majority had looked in vain. The excitement of the past fortnight seemed now wrought up to its highest point and the further details are looked for with increasing interest.

In the days following *Douro*'s return, it soon became clear that a large number of families had lost their primary breadwinner and faced a future of poverty. In some cases, members of the same family had served aboard *Rhone* and sank with her to the bottom of the Caribbean Sea. W. J. Stroud, a forty-six-year-old fore bedroom steward and his thirteen-year-old son, W. J. Stroud Jr., the dispensary boy, both died aboard *Rhone*, leaving Mrs. Stroud alone to care for nine children. Likewise, three members of the Mintram family were lost: John and James Mintram, both twenty-two and presumably twins, along with Alfred Mintram, thirty-six. Henry Bunten, aged twenty-two, and John Bunten, aged fourteen, were also amongst the list of those who never returned.

The concept of a social security system or welfare state was still a hundred years away for British society, leaving bereaved relatives to the mercy of public donations. Fortunately, the more privileged members of Victorian society found fashionable the concept of charity, encouraging the mayor of the Southampton, J. R. Stebbing Esq., to convene a meeting at the town hall on November 25 in order to create a national subscription for survivors and relatives of the deceased. Amongst the dignitaries who attended were Captain Mangles, chairman of the RMSPC; the Right Hon. Russell Gurney, Member of Parliament for the borough; Rear-Admiral Hands; and General Tryon. By the end of the meeting, they had created the West India Hurricane Relief Fund in an effort to alleviate the immediate needs of the bereft.

Within days of the fund being established, a variety of people subscribed various amounts of money and services. The First Hants Voluntary Engineers gave a "grand amateur performance" at their headquarters, and Lord Gerald Fitzgerald tendered the services of his Wandering Minstrels for a charity concert. Individuals such as the Earl of Derby and Mr. G. Moffat MP donated £100 and 100 guineas, respectively, whilst engineers from the Pacific and Orient Company collected the same amount. The crew of the *Douro* all agreed to donate a day's pay, but the principal boost towards validating the fund came from Her Majesty Queen Victoria who, through her secretary, T. M. Biddulph, sent the following message:

Sir, It being understood that a general subscription is about to be raised for the benefit of the widows, orphans and others resident in the United Kingdom who were dependant on those who unhappily lost their lives in the late disastrous hurricane in the West Indies, I am commanded by the Queen to acquaint you, as mayor of Southampton, in which town the misfortune will be more generally felt than elsewhere, that Her Majesty deeply commiserating with those who have been thus deprived of their relatives and of their means of support, desires to subscriber £200 to the fund.

One of the more unusual methods contrived to raise money for the fund involved Colonel Sir Henry James photographing Jonathan Bailey with the life ring that had saved him. He posed in a number of postures, reflecting his experience in the water and subsequent rescue from Beef Island. These images were then printed as *carte de visites* and sold to members of the public curious about Bailey's experience.

Within two days of the fund being initiated, £1,135 had been raised, and the decision was taken to provide bereaved relatives with £3 mourning money each, whilst surviving crew members who had lost their belongings during the catastrophe were given the same amount. Future allocations were dependent on the amount of children involved and the personal circumstances of the family. For example, Amelia Matilda

Jonathan Bailey with fellow surviving cabin boy John Minns (the Royal Society).

Allard, the twenty-five-year-old wife of Clovis Allard, a forty-year-old saloon cook aboard *Rhone*, initially received an immediate payout of £1 with a further mourning allowance of £3. She had three children, one of whom later died and was in fact expecting another when her husband was lost, but this baby later also died. Between December 1867 and May 1868, she received a total of £53 11s (53 pounds, 11 shillings); only £6 9s less than what her husband would have earned on his salary of £10 a month. Elizabeth Ann Andrews, the twenty-six-year-old wife of Quartermaster George Andrews, received considerably less, even though she had three healthy children; however, her husband had only earned £3 10s a month, and she was employed as a washerwoman and mangler, capable of earning her own income. She, consequently, over the six-month period received £37 19s.

Some of the remaining money was used to construct and place a memorial to both *Rhone* and *Wye* victims in the Old Cemetery at Southampton. *The Hampshire Advertiser* described the memorial for its December 1 edition:

> The style is gothic, with some very chaste decorations, and the total height from basement to cross is eighteen feet. The foundation is composed of concrete, upon which is placed a landing of a single Yorkshire stone, somewhat remarkable on account of size, it being nine feet square and six inches thick, and forming therefore a solid basement to the whole structure. Rising from this is a Portland stone landing, upon which stand eight serpentine marble columns, three facing on each quarter—the corners serving two sides—and enclosing on each of the four sides two lancet shaped panel tablets of black marble, the principal ones, which contains the names of Captain Woolley, Mr Dalby Topper (his chief officer), the junior officers, purser, and surgeon, and others—eighteen in all—facing the south.
>
> The pillar caps are carved in water leaves, dolphins, and other marine emblems, the middle one being surmounted by an

upright anchor, the same position over the others being relieved by leaf triplets. Over this there is on the southern side a representation of the steamer *Rhone* carved in white marble, the Wye occupying a similar position on the north side. The east and west quarters contain appropriate texts of scripture, and each is terminated with a pointed gable, its frieze being carved in water lilies. From the whole springs a spire about eight feet high, belted with trefoils etc, and roped up the sides, the whole monument being surmounted with an ornamental metal-gilt cross.

As time passed, the *Rhone* disaster became consigned to memory, remembered only by those who had been fortunate enough to escape from the maelstrom with their lives.

The *Rhone* and *Wye* monument in the Old Cemetery, Southampton (Alamy).

CHAPTER 7

Earthquake and Tsunami

By November in St Thomas, a recovery operation had gathered momentum as salvers and peons slowly cleared the harbour of wreckage that obstructed the incoming traffic carrying relief supplies and food. Many of the inhabitants, having recovered from the initial shock of the storm, laboured incessantly, unaware that more frequently occurring earth tremors may be a precursor to further chaos. Similar operations were taking place on nearby St. Croix where commerce remained suspended, but international diplomacy and intrigue proceeded behind the closed doors of Government House regarding the sale of the island.

At 3:00 p.m. on November 18, in the governor's residence at St. Croix, delegates from the United States and Denmark had gathered to discuss the referendum particulars concerning the purchase of the island by the US government from Denmark when a series of earthquakes occurred, shaking the meeting to a halt. As the local inhabitants fought to navigate through the haze of dust, observers aboard the USS *Monongohela* noticed that, along with the collapse of the English church tower and a number of other buildings, the shoreline had transformed, with much of the harbour seabed now visible whilst the waterline had receded considerably. Some of the older salts aboard the American steamer had observed similar phenomena elsewhere during their careers and looked at one another apprehensively. Gradually, a series of shouts echoed around the ship, each repeating the other, until in one panicked voice the crew screamed unanimously, "Tsunami."

The word tsunami literally translated from the Japanese means harbour wave. These natural leviathans are also sometimes referred to as tidal waves because of their similarity to an incoming tidal bore. Apart from extremely rare variants, tsunamis are caused by either impact events or seismic episodes. By far, the larger of the two are created by impact events that can include meteorite strikes, landslides, or glacial calvings. The 1755 Lisbon earthquake on the Iberian Peninsula created a monstrous wave that spanned the Atlantic in just seven hours, smashing into the Caribbean island of Saba with a height of twenty-two feet and adjacent St. Maarten with a height of fourteen feet.

The most common impetus for the creation of a tsunami involves the tectonic movement of the earth's geological plates, which when grinding against each other occasionally subduct, creating energy released in the form of an earthquake followed by a large wave bore. During the last four hundred years, twenty-three tsunamis have been recorded in the Caribbean region, sixteen of which were created by seismic activity. The Virgin Islands archipelago lies on the eastern tip of the Caribbean plate, the smallest of the fifteen major world plates, with both the North American plate and the South American plate almost encapsulating their inferior counterpart. Some sixty-five million years ago during the Late Cretaceous, early Tertiary period, the North Atlantic plate began subducting under the Caribbean plate, creating the Lesser Antilles Volcanic Arc. The subsequent eruptions that took place formed many of the Lesser Antillean islands, including the Virgin Islands. Tectonic activity is a regular feature of life in the region where typically a number of earthquakes with varying strengths occur every month. October and November 1867, however, were particularly lively months with literally hundreds of tremors.

Curiously, throughout the hurricane of October 29, people in the region felt a series of tremors but ignored their significance due to the tempestuous storm. Captain Vesey's report observed, "Shocks of earthquakes were felt and the electricity was so intense that compasses were useless." Another spectator narrated how "in the town, houses were unroofed and in many cases thrown down by the gale and by three shocks of earthquake which occurred at the same time."

A century earlier, scientists had noticed a regularity with which seismic activity accompanied hurricanes or cyclones and began to hypothesise that a symbiotic interaction could potentially exist between the two. *The Gentleman's Magazine* for 1738–1739 recorded how during the nights of October 11 and 12, 1737, there had been a tempestuous hurricane at the mouth of the Ganges River that travelled for over 150 miles inland. Simultaneously, along the riverbank upon which Calcutta was built, a violent earthquake occurred, collapsing two hundred houses and dislodging the steeple of the Anglican church, which simply sunk into the ground intact. Similar dual disasters had been experienced at Martinique in 1766, Barbados in 1780, Jamaica in 1813, and Tobago in 1847. In August 1837 and 1838, Antigua endured two hurricanes attended with earth tremors, during the first of which "in the midst of the hurricane earthquakes were felt." Whilst still unexplained, scientists have postulated a variety of theorem ranging from seismic shaking to massive changes in atmospheric pressure, including one submitted by meteorologist C. F. Brooks, who in the early 1900s proposed:

> A drop in barometric pressure of two inches removes a load of about two million tons from each square mile of surface, whereas a ten foot rise of water would add about nine million tons to each square mile. The difference, nine million tons of water less two million tons of air pressure, is a possible net result. This effect upon the sea bottom might provide the necessary trigger action to set off the earthquake.

The tremors experienced during the San Narciso hurricane were merely a pre-emptive crescendo of minor shocks building up to a fanfare of eighty-nine earthquakes within a twelve-hour period on November 18. The largest of these quakes, whose epicentre was later estimated to be only fifteen to twenty kilometres away from St. Thomas near Virgin Gorda, prompted a thirty-two-foot vertical displacement on the seafloor, providing the perfect ingredients for an epic wave bore. In describing the event, Mr. Otto Frederick Raupach sent the following description to the secretary of state in Washington:

> The 18th of November was a beautiful clear day, with a fine blue West India sky. There was not the least sign of any kind to foretell this great convulsion in nature, when suddenly, at about quarter of three o'clock in the afternoon, there was heard an underground rumbling noise, which was immediately followed by a terrific earthquake, which seemed to come from south-by-west, and pass on the north-by-east. The earth seemed as if composed of small waves rising and sinking under your feet, so that if you made a step forward, your foot seemed to meet higher ground, and if you put it backward it also there met higher ground. To stand still in one spot was impossible, and when trying to walk it was as if something kept you back. The underground sound, while the first shock was going on, for about one minute and a half, was most dreadful. It terrified every living soul.
>
> The sun seemed at once to become dim; it was as if eclipsed, and this dimness lasted that first day until sunset, and continued the whole of the next day, but in a less degree, and it only wore away entirely in the course of two days more. It was as if the sun, although apparently as bright as usual has lost some of its warming and illuminating power. After the first terrific shock the ground continued groaning and trembling, when about ten minutes after, a second strong shock was felt.
>
> Directly after this second shock the ocean, which shortly before the first shock had receded from the land several hundred feet was seen to rise like one huge wave and come in toward the harbour. It stood up like a straight white wall, about from fifteen to twenty feet high, and advanced very fast into the harbor, sweeping or upsetting small vessels before it, and raising the large men-o-war and steamers to its top. The appearance of this wave was like a white masonry wall erect and straight as if

built with the aid of a rule; it had not the appearance of ordinary waves. It broke in to the lower parts of the town to the height of a couple of feet and to the extent of about two hundred and fifty feet inland, according to the level of the locality. The rising of the waves repeated a second time after an interval of about ten minutes, and the second appeared to be even a little larger than the first, and went a little further inland. After these two waves had passed away, the ocean remained, as far as the eye could see, quite calm again, just as it was before the first shock of the earthquake had occurred.

The shocks continued and were felt every few minutes. It was as if the shocks of the first day hung together in one chain but from 2:45 o'clock on the morning of the 19th of November, the shocks were felt more separately and distinct, and, therefore, seemed as if they were more frequent.

From 2:45 o'clock p.m. on the 18th till 2:45 a.m. on the 19th, there were 89 shocks. From 2:45 o' clock a.m. the 19th till midnight, there were two hundred and thirty eight shocks. The shocks became less severe from the 21st of November.

Other estimates from United States naval personnel calculated the wave at between twenty and twenty-five feet, followed by a continuous succession of aftershocks. Enormous damage was again experienced in Charlotte Amalie with ships being tossed up and thrown ashore. The RMS *La Plata*, which was anchored of Water Island, was almost lost when the wave tore through the bay. Rear Admiral Palmer aboard the flagship USS *Susquehanna* described what he witnessed:

> The English mail steamer which had lately arrived and was coaling in the bay on the other side of the harbour, was as nearly being lost as possible. Her passengers speak of having felt the shock as we did and looking behind them saw a small islet in their rear was cleft in twain, flames and smoke issuing from the

fissure. Shortly afterwards the sea arose and came well nigh carrying them down; their cables parted, but they were thrown most fortunately under a lee which placed them in comparative safety. The passengers, all but three (females) who were lost in the surf, reached the shore.

An *Illustrated London News* lithograph depicting the scene shows the 314-foot vessel taken by the wave and being effortlessly dragged from its anchorage, whilst *Harper's Weekly* provided a vivid description of the passengers' reaction upon sighting the approaching liquid behemoth.

> *La Plata* had a very narrow escape…When the earthquake occurred, it was felt quite as strongly in the ship as ashore. Some thought the boiler had burst; some that the ship was struck by whales…The alarm had scarcely subsided when there was a cry of "its coming, its coming!"…There was a roar like thunder. Captain Revett seized the wheel and endeavoured to present the stern of the ship to the advancing wall; but it struck her on the starboard quarter. Though she reeled, groaned, and staggered with the blow, the wave passed her with no more serious injury than a shattered bulwark and a few tons of salt-water on her deck.

A passenger from *La Plata* who had been ashore observing the damage created by the recent hurricane and was about to return to the ship when the wave arrived survived a remarkable experience.

> We wandered some hours amid the melancholy scene. The day was intensely hot, without a breath of air—quite unseasonable for in ordinary years, fresh easterly winds at this time prevail and the cool air. At about half past 2pm, we started for the wharf, intending to return onboard *La Plata*. We were in the main street, parallel to the shore, when we heard suddenly and without a moments warning, a great roar from seaward. The houses

La Plata riding the tsunami bore (Alamy).

groaned and cracked, the earth heaved, reeled and danced beneath us so that we could scarcely keep our feet. I have been in several earthquakes, but have never felt one of greater intensity, and the inhabitants of St. Thomas, as well as of other islands, declare that they never felt one so severe. Nevertheless, the damage done was not great.

Few, if any houses fell, though probably most were more shaken or cracked. This can only be accounted for by the vertical character of the commotion. Had it been more lateral or gyratory, as many I have experienced, the force was sufficient to have prostrated every house in the town.

Our position in the narrow streets being one of great danger we determined, after a moments consideration, to get onboard the ship. We embarked in a small shore boat, pulled by one local. The shortest way was not by the main entrance, but by a narrow boat channel at the back of Water Island, and for this we steered. We had gone about a quarter of a mile (still in the harbour), when suddenly a strange cry of confusion and fear arose on every side and we saw the crews of various ships and the labourers at work on the wrecks swarming over the sides into small boats and pulling like maniacs for the shore. We were altogether bewildered, but in one moment more the horrible truth broke upon us— the sea was coming in; the great tidal wave, the earthquake, the earthquake "bore" was seen racing shorewards at railway speed.

Our boatman, wild with panic, put round the boat and strained every nerve; and if our race for life had only been with the wave we saw approaching the narrow channel, I think we should have beaten it, checked as it was by the narrowness of the entrance and an outstretching reef; but as we drew into the open harbour we saw the great wall of water far vaster and higher, and ten times as swift, come roaring in upon us. It was not 100 yards from us; I saw a large white schooner at that distance turned bottom upwards as the wave struck her. We still had several yards to make the shore, margined with deep black fetid mud like that which lines the Thames in London. The boatman threw up his oars and plunged overboard, two of our companions instantly followed. I and the remaining one stuck to the boat, hoping that it might be lifted unhurt onto the shore. In another moment we had it—a sort of precursor surf did lift us for a moment, but in a second more the great body of the sea was upon us; the boat broached to, and turned right over. We were buried for some moments in the boiling and fetid mud, the stench of which I shall never forget, but eventually scrambled out and reached the shore through the subsiding wave.

Other vessels crashed onto the shore, totally wrecked, whilst the deluge inundated warehouses and wharves. Meanwhile, at St. Croix, some forty miles away, a young midshipman recently graduated from Annapolis,

Louis Van Housel, was aboard the USS *Monongahela*, an old US wooden warship, when the earthquake struck. Every timber shivered as the vessel was rocked from side to side. Then the sea began to recede.

> By this time the rush of water was towards the ocean. We were carried out perhaps five hundred yards from the shore, when our vessel grounded and the water continuing its retreat, she careened over on her port beams end. The bottom of the roadstead was now visible, nearly bare, for half a mile beyond us, and that immense body of water which had covered the bay and part of the town was reforming with the whole Atlantic as an ally, for a tremendous charge upon us and the shore. This was the supreme moment of the catastrophe. As far as the eye could reach to the north and to the south was a high threatening wall of green water. It seemed to pause for a moment, as if marshalling its strength, and then on it came in a majestic unbroken column, more awe inspiring than an army with banners. The suspense was terrible. Our noble vessel seemed as a tiny nutshell to withstand the shock of the mighty rushing Niagara that was advancing upon us. Many a hasty prayer was uttered by lips unused to devotion. All expected to be engulfed, and but a few had any hope of surviving.

The *Monongahela* was carried onto the shore and beached between some rocks. From there, her ship's complement used ropes to scramble down the hull and then ran towards high ground. A Spanish brig, which had been picked up by the wave and carried onshore, stood upright on the King's Highway, blocking the road, whilst many buildings had simply collapsed into the street. When the wave began to recede back to the sea, it carried an assortment of flotsam: "This water bore on its surface all manner of debris which it gathered from the yards and houses in its course: chairs, cradles, bedsteads, broken fences, and doors; together with flocks of ducks and geese quacking and gabbing, utterly bewildered by the sudden rise of their element."

Meanwhile, the British islands had likewise received the full force of the tsunami bore that tore through the Sir Francis Drake Channel. On Salt Island, where occasional wreckage from the *Rhone* still drifted ashore, the wave blasted through a gap in the hillside at South Bay, hauling debris with it and spewing it either side before bursting across the salt pond and then washing the settlement, with its accompanying houses, into the sea. Fissures opened up close to the shoreline through which water spurted, an anomaly likewise observed at Tortola, adding further to the infernal scene.

On Virgin Gorda, the blocks of granite that litter the southwest tip of the island "were rent during the first shocks," whilst on Peter Island, believing that the sudden rise in water level would result in the consumption of their island, the inhabitants jumped into any available boat and raced across to Tortola. The earthquake shocks and tsunami compounded the damage created by the preceding hurricane, leaving every stone building affected to some degree, whilst ramshackle piles of lumber littering the hillsides were all that remained of the wooden shacks that the majority of the inhabitants had lived in. Arthur Rumbold, president of the Virgin Islands, was forced to draft another melancholy report to his direct superior in Antigua in which he lamented further catastrophic events.

> Sir—I have to report to Your Excellency that on the 18th instant the Virgin Islands was visited by a severe earthquake which lasted fully fifteen minutes and was followed by numerous other shocks less severe not exceeding five minutes, for over twelve hours; repeated shocks still occur, all appear to come from the north or north-west, save the first which came from the north-east.
>
> Immediately after the first shock had ceased, the sea receded or rather sunk about four and five feet above its original level, submerging the whole of the lowest part of the town, sweeping before it nearly all the smaller dwellings which had not been entirely destroyed by the late hurricane and had been replaced in their original positions.

On the sea rising an excessively strong current set in, first towards the land, then seaward, the first tide and current threw up a quantity of deposit from the sea with a strong sulphurous smell, from the velocity with which the old lumber and other matters were taken along by the current first in one direction and then another, I should say that it was running at the rate of at least twelve knots. The inhabitants of the town betook themselves for safety from the overflowing tide to the side of the hill, where some whose houses had been at first much injured by the hurricane and subsequently by the earthquakes, still remain under canvas or shed fixed up of dry grass.

Whilst affecting the Virgin Islands most directly, the tsunami bore disseminated throughout the Caribbean, greeting Guadeloupe with a thirty-two-foot-high wave, with other smaller inundations spreading as far south as Isla de Margarita, five hundred miles away. An idea of the speed this particular bore travelled may be established by the fact that it reached Trinidad 560 miles away from the Virgin Islands within two hours of the main quake.

Within the short space of less than a month, the Virgin Islands had experienced three of nature's worst manifestations: a category-three sustained hurricane, followed by a strong local earthquake, which subsequently created a twenty-five-foot tsunami bore. Rear Admiral Palmer of the USS *Susquehanna* in a letter to the secretary of the navy in Washington reported:

> The damage on the shore has been far more ruinous to the merchants than that occasioned by the late hurricane. The first heavy roller went up into the town, swamping the stores which were mostly on the bay front, floating out, and finally stranding their goods in unheard of directions.
>
> The panic that seized the inhabitants was painful. Rushing up the hillsides and crying for mercy and listening to no attempt

to pacify them. As I went ashore in the evening I found all the stone dwellings were abandoned, their owners either in the streets or the wooden buildings of their friends; the alarm still being kept up by the constant shocks still occurring.

The devastation was so absolute it prompted an observer to predict, "St. Thomas will never recover from this blow." Such an important commercial hub could not, however, be allowed to disintegrate, so an immediate response to the situation initially addressed the submerged wrecks blocking the harbour. Within weeks, salvage teams had arrived and began the grisly task of recovering bodies from the wrecks, along with any items of value, before setting charges to demolish the submerged hulks.

After the tsunami in St. Thomas harbour (Alamy).

CHAPTER 8

Salvage and Rediscovery

THE CLOSING WEEKS of 1867 presaged a bleak future for the inhabitants of the Virgin Islands who, having been ransacked by nature's indiscriminate fury, had little reason to celebrate the approaching holiday season. In contrast, the opening months of the following year witnessed a concerted effort to repair the infrastructure so necessary for the commercial survival of St. Thomas, which, for two centuries, had provided a vital economic hub for Denmark in the Western Hemisphere.

From the outset, the philosophy for colonizing St. Thomas revolved around trading ambitions. Whilst plantation agriculture was marginally practiced on the island, the main occupation involved shipping basic Danish goods to the port of Charlotte Amalie and then exchanging them for plantation products, a luxury in Europe and, consequently, very profitable. The Danish ability to remain neutral during the persistent European conflicts of the eighteenth century contributed to the success of St. Thomas throughout this period (apart from sporadic interruptions), providing an unencumbered reliable location for vessels to conduct secure commerce. Throughout the nineteenth century, shipping from a variety of nations regularly converged in the bay surrounding the town of Charlotte Amalie, disgorging valuable freight into the cavernous warehouses that dominated the shoreline wharves. Smaller vessels would then be loaded with European and American products for redistribution throughout the Eastern Caribbean, making St. Thomas a mercantile centre in the region.

Civil unrest at neighbouring St. Croix during 1848 had essentially forced Governor Von Scholten to emancipate the remaining enslaved population, but by then the plantation economy had virtually collapsed. Consequently in 1868, it was vital for the survival of St. Thomas that the harbour be swiftly cleared of hurricane and tsunami wreckage in order to perpetuate the maritime trade upon which the island relied. To accomplish this, helmet divers were recruited to salvage whatever valuables remained inside the twisted hulks and then set charges to destroy them and unblock the anchorage. Soon after 1867, an eccentric diver from Countmasherry, County Cork, Ireland, named Jeremiah Dennis Murphy arrived at St. Thomas with his two brothers, where he was to remain for three years salvaging wrecks in Charlotte Amalie harbour.

A pioneering character, Murphy started diving Caribbean wrecks just sixteen years after Augustus Siebe had invented the closed-diving helmet. Having immigrated to Boston in the late 1840s, where he trained as a helmet diver, Murphy became involved with a treasure-seeking company who wished to use the Turks and Caicos Islands as their base in the West Indies. Murphy arrived on Grand Turk in 1856, and three years later was based in Jamaica, cleaning and repairing Royal Navy ships in Kingston Harbour. Whilst working on HMS *Valorous* in 1859, he took time to dive on the submerged city of Port Royal and was probably the first to do so.

The Spanish founded Port Royal, the original capital of Jamaica, in 1518. In 1655, during Oliver Cromwell's grand design, the island was captured by the English, after which Port Royal grew to a town with two thousand dwellings and some sixty-five hundred inhabitants. Estimated to have one tavern for every fourteen people, Port Royal served as a notorious hideout for pirates such as Henry Morgan and Blackbeard.

At 11:43 a.m. on June 7, 1692, a tremendous earthquake rocked the island, submerging most of Port Royal and its inhabitants. The ensuing tsunami created further mayhem, consuming many of the people who had survived the initial shock. Subsequently, the town was abandoned to the sea, and a new capital, Kingston, built across the harbour. Although the presence of the submerged municipality was known and parts of it were visible from the surface on calm days, it was Murphy who provided the first account of the site, which he sent to the *Falmouth Post*.

> I first went down on the remains of old Port Royal on the 28th of August, and found that what I had heard with regard to some of the buildings being seen when the water was clear was correct. I landed among the remains of ten or more houses, the walls of which were from three to ten feet above the sand. The day was rather cloudy and I could only get a view of a small portion at a time.
>
> About 12 0'clock (being down four hours) the water cleared a little, and getting a clearer view I concluded that the ruins which I was on must have been those of a fort. But soon after I found a large granite stone somewhat the same shape and size as a tombstone, which was covered with a coral formation, so I could not tell whether it had an inscription or not. Fancying this stone to have been a tombstone, thereby indicating the vicinity of a churchyard, I was not satisfied what the character of the building could have been.
>
> I am of opinion, from what I have seen of old Port Royal, that many of the houses remained perfect after the earthquake, though sunk in the water, and that the sand has been thrown up, and the mud settled around and in them from time to time, until all but the largest buildings are covered over, so the remains of the houses which I have seen may have been the top part of the highest buildings; which is apparently the case from the irregularity of the heights.

Murphy eventually found his way to St. Thomas where he and his two brothers spent the closing years of the 1860s clearing the wreckage in Charlotte Amalie harbour. Meanwhile, the Virgin Islands superintendent for the Royal Mail Steam Packet Company, Mr. J. B. Cameron, had turned his attention to *Rhone*, whose stern section still stood proud of the water, wedged upon Black Rock Point. Initial newspaper reports had stated that *Rhone* carried no gold or species, which was not entirely true. Like all mail ships, *Rhone* carried a significant sum aboard, which the RMSPC desperately needed in order to finance reconstruction of its facilities at Charlotte Amalie. Murphy was dispatched to Salt Island where he began stripping the wreck. Sometime in May 1870, Murphy was visited by friends who in a letter to the *Port of Spain Gazette* in Trinidad gave a detailed account of his activities on the *Rhone* wreck site.

> We paid a visit to the Murphys about two weeks ago, they are at Salt Island diving various things out of the wreck of the steamer *Rhone*. I have never seen a diving dress, it was a novelty to all of us; the children were delighted to see Murphy in his dress, he certainly cut an awful figure, but when he went overboard and we saw him sinking, sinking until we lost sight of him, it was something horrible—the water is 17 fathoms and you can't see the bottom—he was gone for hours, he sent up 12 bales of cotton and various other things: amongst other matters, a fine skull, which must have belonged to a very large man—the cotton is as good as the day it went down; he also saved the anchors and chains and lots of copper.
>
> While he was down he sent a message up to invite the ladies down into the saloon of the *Rhone*. I took a slice of lamb over and we had a first rate dinner. When dinner was nearly ready, Murphy came up, rested for a few minutes and said. "Now ladies, as I have nothing good to offer you, I will take a look into the other half of the ship (she is broken in two pieces) and see what can be got." They begged him not to go but he went and in half an hour we had as much champagne, beer and soda water, lemonade, seltza water and brandy as we knew what to do with, the liquors were as good as they were the first day and it is nearly three years since they have been down; the champagne was first rate, as cool as possible, we drank it out of tumblers as we did

not have champagne glasses. The Murphy's, (three brothers of them) came to St. Thomas soon after the hurricane of 1867 and have been there ever since.

When the *Rhone* was wrecked they saved the species and bullion out of her and got a large sum of money from Mr. Cameron, some $20,000 for their part, the steamer had on board some £60,000 in species and bullion. A few months ago the second brother was drowned in St. Thomas harbour, he went down into the hold of the Liverpool Packet and by some means something went wrong and the poor fellow was drowned; the two remaining brothers felt his loss very much. Murphy tells me he sees an enormous Jewfish in the saloon of the *Rhone*, but the fellow won't come near him.

Much of what the two brothers salvaged was later publicly auctioned, but tragically, Murphy's second brother died during a dive soon after, leaving Jeremiah alone and mourning. With his contracts completed, the surviving Murphy returned to Turks and Caicos, taking with him one item he had kept from *Rhone*'s salvage. Until recently, the whereabouts of *Rhone*'s large bronze bell had remained a mystery until it was located at the top of the steeple tower at St. Georges Church in South Caicos. Murphy, a staunch Anglican, had recovered the bell and then donated it to the church where it still calls the faithful to service every Sunday.

Once the Murphys had finished salvaging *Rhone*, she became forgotten about and consigned to the list of unfortunate ships that had abruptly finished operating before their time. Portsmouth-based painter William Frederick Mitchell illustrated the ship listing heavily to starboard whilst steaming for the open sea. Mitchell earned his living illustrating Brassey's *Naval Annual*, but officers and crew members also engaged him to immortalise their former vessels, and it may have been a survivor or relative who commissioned this watercolour, which eventually found its way to the National Maritime Museum in Greenwich, London. In comparison to other shipwrecks that occurred during the same period, the *Rhone* disaster was not considered a particularly heavy loss of life. For example, *The Princess Alice*, a twin-side paddle pleasure steamer built alongside *Rhone*'s sister ship *Douro* at Caird and Company during 1865, was run down on the River Thames by the collier *Bywell Castle* in 1878 with the loss of 640 lives in a matter of minutes.

As time passed by, the only people to remember what had happened on that late October afternoon were the Salt Islanders who had experienced the event and maintained the humble graveyard where some of the unfortunate passengers and crew were interred. This small cemetery is located away from the local settlement and separate to the islander's family graves. Enclosed within a loose stone circular wall just a few meters from the rocky shoreline, nine distinct graves can be identified, guarded by two palm trees. Two of these graves contain the remains of Chief Officer Dalby Topper and barman Samuel Daly. A photograph taken of the Salt Island community twenty years after the storm of 1867 shows a group of well-dressed Virgin Islanders, many of whom would have remembered the day when the pride of the RMSPC was torn apart on their island.

The *Rhone* cemetery on Salt Island (Junior Daniel).

As the twentieth century progressed, people began viewing the Caribbean region not as an economic plantation entity, but as a pristine series of islands the clear azure waters and year-round warmth of which presented an ideal location for a vacation. During the mid-1930s, a writer named Desmond Holdridge visited the region, stopping briefly at Salt Island where, upon landing, he found a community that had changed little in the preceding years since the *Rhone* disaster and who maintained a strong memory of the incident, perpetuated through the oral tradition. Upon interviewing a Salt Islander about his home, Holdridge was given a detailed account of the *Rhone*, spoken in the vernacular dialect that he subsequently translated to text.

Dere have a drownded ship on de odder side of de island. She lost in de gale of '67. She come out of Great Harbour, in Peter Island, dat de next cay, an' de gale was blowing full force. An' it were two o'clock in de ah'ternoon time, but it were dark like midnight when it have no moon and de Capting didn't see a t'ing an' de gale took possession of de ship, an' drive she back faster dan de engine drive she ahaid, an' she go up on de Black Rock an' mash up, an' fall back in de deep water an' drownded.

De mos' of de bodies dey find on de Tortola shore. Dey bury dem where dey come ashore but a few came ashore here an' de people dat was saved was pile up by de sea an' trow up over de rocks an' den blow back into de island. Later on, a mon come out an' dynamite de hull an' dive down lookin' for gold. An' a mon-of-war come an' dere was trouble for some of de colored people dat stole de rings an' bracelets from de dead people. But only a few, most of them were scared to touch de bodies.

After the Second World War, adventurous sailors began exploring the Caribbean islands on small private boats and writing travelogues about their experiences. George Eggleston visited the Leeward Islands during the late 1950s. In 1959, he published a book entitled *Virgin Islands*.

He mentions stopping at Salt Island and asking an "old man in white dungarees and a tattered black coat" about *Rhone*. After enquiring as to her whereabouts, Eggleston was told, "Yessuh, de wreck on de sout' side. My faddah he help bury some ob de corpses here. Many, many, many peoples drownded."

Throughout the 1960s, considerable economic changes took place in the Virgin Islands, with particular interest focusing on tourism development targeted towards the American market. With Cuba shut to American tourists after the embargo, a new Caribbean destination was required with the most obvious choice being Puerto Rico. There was, however, a language barrier during a period when few Puerto Ricans spoke English, leading travel agents and investors to scrutinise the United States Virgin Islands (USVI) as a potential alternative. In anticipation, the government of the USVI created the Tourist Development Board in 1952, signalling their intent to concentrate on this new and growing industry.

During the 1950s, St. Thomas rapidly evolved into a Caribbean playground for American tourists who, as predicted, migrated to the new Caribbean destination. In 1949, just sixteen thousand tourists had visited the USVI which, subsequent to the Cuban issue, spiked to 164,000 in 1959. This exponential growth recorded 1,122,317 visitors by 1969, providing an impetus for extending the same product to the adjacent British islands. A significant boost to this aspiration materialised in the form of Laurance Rockefeller who, whilst sailing past Virgin Gorda in the late 1950s, spotted a golden beach in the shape of a crescent that he nicknamed Wilderness Beach. Rockefeller, considered one of the pioneers of ecotourism, had in 1956 under the umbrella of his resort management company Rockresorts, opened a luxury retreat on nearby St. John named Caneel Bay and aspired to do the same on Virgin Gorda. In 1958, Rockefeller purchased the land abounding the beach he had targeted, and over the next six years constructed an avant-garde resort christened Little Dix Bay, the original name for the area, which had been dedicated to its owner during the plantation era, one George Dix.

In 1964, Little Dix Bay opened its doors, heralding the birth of British Virgin Islands' tourism, which conveniently coincided with the evolution of a new recreational sport, today known as scuba diving.

Throughout the 1950s, Jacques Cousteau and Emile Gagnan, inventors of the aqualung, began exporting their creation internationally providing amateurs with equipment that enabled them to breathe underwater, something previously only reserved for the military. In 1958, an adventurous American from Massachusetts, Herbert Francis Kilbride, dived *Rhone*, probably for the first time since the Murphy brothers had salvaged the wreck some ninety years earlier. Bert, as he was more popularly known, began salvaging the remaining artefacts from the wreck site, including hundreds of bottles and one of the signal cannons that he later placed in a display at Saba Rock Island in North Sound, Virgin Gorda; a small islet he had purchased to develop into a bar for the growing number of diving visitors finding their way to the Virgin Islands.

Bert Kilbride with some of the artefacts he salvaged from *Rhone* (Eva Baskin).

Another Virgin Islands scuba pioneer, George Marler, who operated Aquatic Centres on Tortola, likewise promoted and regularly dived *Rhone*. The story of the *Rhone* being forced out to sea had particularly fascinated George, and in February 1974, he decided to track down the lost anchor. Having secured his dive boat on the Bank Reef outside of Great Harbour, Peter Island, George descended to the seabed where he immediately started to see bottles and other artefacts. Based on the fact that this was a regular anchorage for RMSPC vessels, the likelihood of finding material dropped from their ships was high on the basis that littering was not considered a social crime in the nineteenth century. Knowing that he was in the right vicinity, George continued to search until he found the abandoned anchor with the chain still attached.

It was in July 1977 that *Rhone* reached international attention when her submerged hulk was used as a set during the production of Peter Yates's film *The Deep*. Based on the book by Peter Benchley who had introduced *Jaws* to the world two years earlier, *The Deep* tells the story of a young couple played by Nick Nolte and Jacqueline Bisset who, whilst vacationing in Bermuda, stumble across a shipwreck named the *Goliath*, laden with ampoules of morphine. Underneath this wreck lies an older eighteenth century Spanish shipwreck laden with treasure and in particular, a jewel-encrusted gold necklace that provides royal provenance for the mystery vessel.

Jacqueline Bisset, Nick Nolte, and Robert Shaw filming the 1977 movie *The Deep* (Alamy).

Much of the underwater location footage was filmed around the bow section of *Rhone*, including the memorable scene where Jacqueline Bisset's character (Gail Berke) is dragged by the arm into the wreck by a giant green moray eel (*Gymnothorax funebris*). In order to stage this particular stunt, Jackie Kilbride (wife of Bert Kilbride) doubled for Bisset, and a diver was placed inside the wreck with a piece of rope. At the appointed time, Kilbride held on to the rope whilst the diver pulled vigorously from the other side. Unfortunately, the overenthusiastic diver jerked so hard on the rope that Kilbride's arm was badly dislocated; however, the scene was considered so realistic that it was wrapped in one take.

The gradual development of tourism in the BVI encouraged more dive operations to open whose owners eventually formed a mutually beneficial organisation known as the Dive Ops Society. Around the same time in 1980, the National Parks Trust of the BVI recognised the damage being done to the wreck site by random anchoring so declared *Rhone* a protected national park, the boundaries for which extend as far as Dead Chest Island. In total, the park covers almost eight hundred acres within which fishing and interference of the wreck site is illegal.

Black Rock Point today (Junior Daniel).

In 1986, George Marler sold his Aquatic Centres to a colourful character named Alan Baskin who, with his wife Eva, opened Baskin in the Sun. Through Alan's connections with the Rotary Club of Tortola, a sum of $30,000, donated by Swedish entrepreneur Mr. Bengt Nygren, was used to install the first mooring balls on the wreck site. In 1991, the National Parks trust installed a series of mooring balls over the site for dive boats, charter boats, and dinghies, which were monitored and maintained by staff from their boat *Rhone Ranger*. This mooring system is presently still in operation and provides a safe, nonintrusive means to secure vessels above the wreck site whilst allowing easy access for scuba divers and snorkelers.

CHAPTER 9

The Wreck Site Today

TODAY, THE WRECK site of RMS *Rhone* is divided into three main sections that rest at between eighty-four and twelve feet deep. The bow section is the deepest of the three, at an average of seventy feet, whilst what has generally been recognised as a condenser lies at eighty-four feet. The stern section is the second largest remaining portion of the vessel, resting on an incline between thirty-four and sixty feet underwater, whilst in between lies the midsection, which is a dispersed assemblage of debris lying at between fifty to seventy-two feet beneath the surface. The stern post is the shallowest part of the wreck and, at just twelve feet from the surface, is well within range of snorkelers.

The bow section of the *Rhone* resting on the starboard side (Armando Jenik).

The wreck site has changed dramatically since October 29, 1867, through both natural and unnatural interference. The day after the wrecking, both the stern section and the foremast stood above the surface. This is not the case today.

Popular myth alleges that either the American or British navy detonated charges on the wreck site due to her being a navigation hazard sometime during the 1950s to 1960s. Certainly, the British Royal Navy has no record of this taking place, and the American navy cannot legally enter British waters and start randomly detonating charges close to a community of Her Majesty's subjects. This could potentially have created a diplomatic incident that would have proved embarrassing for both countries. Local residents who were alive during the 1950s and 1960s have no recollection of the stern being above the water or anybody blowing it up.

According to the *Port of Spain Gazette*, Jeremiah Murphy blew the ship open in order to access the bullion room, which would have been located close to the engine room. He recovered the safe, which apparently contained around £60,000. It is evident when looking at the stern section of *Rhone* that charges were placed inside the wreckage, then when detonated, blew the hull open and outwards, destroying the engine room and simple inverted two-cylinder engine. The powerful explosion lifted the stern off Black Rock Point and threw it underwater, giving the impression that far more damage occurred during the wrecking process than in fact did, and giving rise to the incorrect myth that the boilers had exploded on impact with the seawater.

The boilers had explosives placed inside of them, but just enough to blow them open and expose the copper tubing that would have lined the pipes to prevent saltwater corrosion. The *Port of Spain Gazette* report clearly states that Murphy had recovered copper, suggesting he was responsible for the subsequent boiler damage. The two midsections lying either side of the stern section are also a casualty of Murphy's work and would have been attached to the stern section subsequent to sinking. This suggests that a massive explosion took place during the salvage process. Although the damage is extensive in the area of the engine room, elements of the mechanics are still visible, including the propeller, which is virtually intact, apart from some damage to one of the three blades. Also lying at a depth between thirty-nine and forty-six feet, almost parallel to the propeller shaft, is the aft mast.

Clearly as extensions of the engine room, the two midsections contain artefacts including a series of large wrenches used by the ship's engineers and a water pump employed to feed the thirsty boilers and ship's plumbing. Further debris surrounds these portions, including a relatively intact boiler, the interior piping of which has been exposed, probably again by Murphy when he retrieved any remaining copper.

Whilst the stern section has been altered by unnatural events subsequent to sinking, alternatively, the bow section appears to have just keeled over to the starboard side where it rests fully submerged with the forward mast still stepped into the hull, lying at a right angle. An initial hypothesis of the wreck site formation would suggest that the tsunami that followed the hurricane of 1867 may have been responsible for toppling over the foremast and bow section. Certainly this wave of destruction reached Salt Island, as former local resident Nora Smith-Manse remembers as a child being told that the tsunami left hundreds of dead fish in the salt pond and swept large chunks of coral inland where they still remain today. The destruction created by the enormous wave was so complete that many Salt Islanders evacuated their ancestral home and never returned. Unfortunately, this theory of the wreck site must be discounted on the basis that an account survives of the mast still remaining above the water at around the same time that Murphy salvaged the wreck. Charles Kingsley, who visited the Caribbean in the early 1870s and, subsequently, in 1871, published an account of his experience entitled *At Last: A Christmas in the West Indies*, writing that:

> The clear air, the still soft outlines, the rich and yet delicate colouring, stir up a sense of purity and freshness, and peace and cheerfulness, such as is stirred up by certain views of the

Mediterranean and its shores, only broken by one ghastly sight, the lonely mast of the ill fated *Rhone*, standing up still where she sank with all her crew, in the hurricane of 1867.

Based on this account, it could not have been the tsunami of November 1867 that capsized the mast and bow section. Consequently, it must be assumed that a later hurricane such as the Gale of '24 (1924) may have been responsible for pushing the mast and bow section over, or that the iron hull plating corroded underwater and then collapsed, dropping the mast and hull onto the starboard side.

The depth to the port-side hull of the bow section at its shallowest is fifty-three feet, whilst the keel at the bow rests at seventy-five feet. Due to the intact nature of the bow, divers are able to swim through the wreckage, providing one of the most visually stunning experiences available in the world of recreational scuba diving. Most tour leaders enter the bow section of *Rhone* just forward from where the funnel was located through a large opening created when the ship parted and sank. One of two cannons known to have been aboard can be seen close to the entrance beneath the iron deck support beams, which point to the surface. These guns were redundant in the Caribbean, but in the English Channel, where thick fog had been the cause of many collisions, they would have served as signal guns alerting other vessels to *Rhone*'s presence.

Inside of the cavernous hulk, divers weave through the tangled wreckage of deck support beams in an area that contained second-class cabins and crew quarters, then exit next to the mast, which still has the crow's nest at the top. The deepest element of the wreck site, known as the condenser, rests at eighty-four feet on the seabed and is usually surrounded by shoals of fish, in particular, squirrel fish (*Holocentrus adscensionis*).

In addition to the wreck itself, the abundant sea life also attracts recreational divers due to the diverse cornucopia of marine creatures that gather in an unusually small area. Along with the myriad of fish

The *Rhone*'s cannon pointing out through the wreckage (Armando Jenik).

Squirrel fish gathering around the condenser (Armando Jenik).

that inhabit the site, hawksbill turtles (*Eretmochelys imbricata*) occasionally amble past whilst harmless Nurse sharks drift sleepily through the mangled ironwork. The presence of *Rhone* has created a unique ecosystem that would be absent if not for the protective nooks and crannies the wreck site provides the many marine creatures that occupy it.

A Nurse shark drifting through the wreckage (Armando Jenik).

Economically, the presence of *Rhone* contributes significantly towards employing a large number of people whose livelihoods in part rely on the reputation and accessibility of the internationally famous shipwreck. Some twenty dive operations located in the British Virgin Islands and United States Virgin Islands ferry guests daily to Black Rock Point, offering both scuba and snorkel tours, usually highlighted with their own spectacular account of what happened on that dark afternoon in October 1867. They are supplemented by private charter boat operators and bareboat or independent skippers, whose numbers have never been accurately recorded but must run into thousands each year, making *Rhone* the most visited historical site in the modern territory.

This popularity has implanted *Rhone* firmly within the promotional identity of the BVI, especially amongst the tourism sector. A variety of media expose this unique cultural resource including official stamps, the first of which was designed in 1970 by John Waddington as part of a series entitled Ships with Historic Links to the Caribbean and the Virgin Islands, featuring *Rhone* as depicted in William Frederick Mitchell's painting. In 1984, *Rhone* again featured within a series of four stamps produced to commemorate the 250th anniversary of the *Lloyd's List*. Three years later in 1987, John Batchelor created a new image amongst a series entitled Shipwrecks depicting *Rhone* at full steam fighting against the storm, showing her starboard bow. All three of these stamps were widely distributed internationally. Subsequently, in 2000, the BVI Olympic Committee used *Rhone*'s familiar profile to feature on one of their official pins, providing further global exposure for an already iconic destination.

Whilst the economic benefits created by *Rhone*'s presence are obviously positive, a question slowly gathering momentum is what negative impact on the wreck site itself is all of this activity generating? Most operators who provide tours follow the same route with only slight variations, the most popular segment of which takes divers through the bow section in an overhead environment. As each individual exhales though their regulator, pockets of air become trapped in the hull, creating unnatural aerobic spaces, which over the course of time may affect the structural integrity of that particular portion. Inevitably, to guarantee the perpetuity of *Rhone*, a multidimensional survey must take place of the wreck site studying a variety of elements, including diver movements and their consequential effects. Should potentially compromised areas be identified, symbiotic supportive elements could be introduced that strengthen the corroding iron hull appropriately.

Likewise, a detailed study recording each individual feature of the wreck site would provide an unparalleled insight into post-mid-nineteenth-century steamship technology during a period that saw rapid and ingenious engineering development. Whilst *Rhone*'s demise, salvage, and surroundings have all taken their individual toll on the remaining iron carcass, significant propulsion elements remain, including most noticeably the propeller, the propeller shaft, and gearbox, all of which, in accordance to her owner's wishes, would have been the best available at the time.

The *Rhone*'s propeller (Armando Jenik).

The iron rudder, wedged at an acute angle to its original position and almost intact, displays a noticeably more evolved profile than that of the wooden relic that steered the SS *Great Britain* completed just twenty years earlier. The wreck site itself will inevitably provide a unique resource for steamship enthusiasts when studied under the jurisdiction of the National Parks Trust by trained maritime/nautical archaeologists.

Although a nascent academic discipline until recently, maritime or nautical archaeology has grown swiftly, providing fascinating insights into submerged vessels. In 1960, George Bass, an archaeologist working with Texas A&M University, became the first person to completely excavate a shipwreck at Cape Gelidonya near Finike in Turkey. Bass initiated a new archaeological discipline that has grown into a fertile area of research, not least because organic items that would normally deteriorate on land remain preserved underwater. Probably the most outstanding example are the English longbows recovered from the *Mary Rose* when she was raised from the Solent in 1982. Prior to her discovery, there were only a few surviving longbows in poor condition until the Tudor warship yielded 137 intact examples, providing data previously unavailable for this defining medieval weapon. Whilst countless artefacts have been salvaged from *Rhone*, many remain, which if conserved properly and combined with what has already been officially collected, would provide a substantial assemblage towards a spectacular museum exhibit.

A further application for *Rhone* encompassed within a much larger socioeconomic project would include her being a major display component for a potential Salt Island Interpretation Centre. Described in March 1711 as being "so called for the vast quantities of salt it generally produces every year," the value of Salt Island was recognised early. Robert Dinwiddie, writing in April 1740, observed that Salt Island produced "large quantities of salt which has proved of great use to the British Northern colonies on the continent of America." Salt has always remained highly prized throughout human history, being decisive in the rise and decline of a number of civilisations. Economically, the value of salt has usually remained consistent, leading to its use in some cultures as a currency. Roman soldiers, for example, sometimes received their pay in salt, and the word *salary* is derived from *sal*, the Latin for *salt*. Consequently, if Legionnaires fought hard they were considered "worth their salt."

The large but shallow ponds located on Salt Island encompass an area approximately twenty-three acres in size; they attracted early settlers who created a community that thrived for almost two centuries. The figures for 1815 record thirty-one residents, which by 1823 had jumped to 119, most of whom were classified as free blacks who were concentrating on a growing fishing industry and harvesting twenty-seven hundred bushels of salt to corn their catch. Following freedom in 1834 and the subsequent collapse of the plantation system, more newly emancipated people began to migrate to Salt Island, which became a focal point for the contiguous sister islands. The shift towards industrialisation, motivated by tourism in the early 1970s, encouraged many Salt Islanders to relocate, most of whom became residents on Tortola, abandoning their traditional settlement.

Although now derelict, the small village on the shoreline of Lee Bay becomes rejuvenated each year as dozens of Salt Islanders return and celebrate their unique heritage with a barbeque and fun day. Many of the younger members of this proud group harbour ambitions to revitalise their ancestral home, and if an interpretation centre were constructed that exhibited both their history and the *Rhone*, more visitors would be encouraged to come, facilitating the construction of bars, restaurants, and shops owned and operated by Salt Islanders.

Whatever her future, put simply, the wreck site of RMS *Rhone* is a unique cultural resource not replicated anywhere else underwater. Whilst other steamships sank during the same period, none are more intact and as accessible to both scuba divers and snorkelers. What was considered in the late 1860s to be a Victorian tragedy has unfolded into a veritable treasure for the modern inhabitants of the BVI; the *Rhone* draws thousands of visitors each year, and in essence was responsible for initiating the recreational diving industry in the modern territory—today a multimillion dollar business. Had *Rhone* completed her career as the owners had intended, she would have eventually been unceremoniously dismantled in an obscure yard, like hundreds of her colleagues, before drifting into the annals of steamship history, whilst her crew members would be long forgotten and unheralded. By sinking on that fateful day in October 1867, however, *Rhone* has assured her place in maritime folklore. For generations to come, she will act as a magnet to visitors who wish to explore possibly the most exciting shipwreck to be found anywhere in the world.

A diver exploring the wreck of the *Rhone* (Alamy).

Sources

The most accessible firsthand information concerning the Virgin Islands hurricane of 1867 may be found in the numerous contemporary broadsheets that syndicated the story throughout the English-speaking world, amongst which the *Illustrated London News* reported most extensively. More provincial newspapers based in the Southampton area, such as the *Hampshire Chronicle*, interviewed survivors personally, but only some of their accounts reached a wider audience. Throughout the closing months of 1867 as more information became available, both newspapers regularly reported on the incident and it is from these that the eyewitness accounts were gleaned.

The National Maritime Museum has records concerning the Royal Mail Steam Packet Company, but these are mostly kept in a separate storage facility and must be ordered to the reading room well in advance. Much of the material relating to the RMSPC was destroyed during the London blitz, so any ship's plans or technical data for *Rhone* is probably lost. The Hampshire Records Office in Southampton retains a considerable amount of material relating to more practical affairs, including the accounts for the survivors and widows' funds.

Three books describing the events surrounding *Rhone's* loss were referenced including George and Luana Marler's book *The Royal Mail Steamer Rhone*, Andrew C. Jampoler's *Black Rock and Blue Water*, and Stephen Ashley's *Hurricane Earthquake Tidal Wave*.

There is more out there, though, and with any luck this publication will encourage others to search more thoroughly for information about this fascinating ship.

Copies of the paintings by George Wilkinson may be purchased from: www.nauticalart.ca

CPSIA information can be obtained
at www.ICGtesting.com
Printed in the USA
LVHW07n1817240918
591186LV00019B/724/P